seated *with Christ*

seated *with Christ*

LIVING FREELY
IN A CULTURE OF COMPARISON

heather holleman

MOODY PUBLISHERS

CHICAGO

All Scripture quotations, unless otherwise indicated, are taken from the Holy Bible, New International Version®, NIV®. Copyright © 1973, 1978, 1984, 2011 by Biblica, Inc.™ Used by permission of Zondervan. All rights reserved worldwide. www.zondervan.com. The "NIV" and "New International Version" are trademarks registered in the United States Patent and Trademark Office by Biblica, Inc.™

Scripture quotations marked NLT are taken from the Holy Bible, New Living Translation, copyright © 1996, 2004, 2007, 2013 by Tyndale House Foundation. Used by permission of Tyndale House Publishers, Inc., Carol Stream, Illinois 60188. All rights reserved.

Scripture quotations marked ESV are from The Holy Bible, English Standard Version® (ESV®), copyright © 2001 by Crossway, a publishing ministry of Good News Publishers. Used by permission.

All rights reserved. Published in association with the literary agency of D.C. Jacobson and Associates LLC, 537 SE Ash Street, Suite 203, Portland, OR 97214.

Edited by Pam Pugh
Author photo: BowerShots Photography
Interior design: Ragont Design
Cover design: Erik M. Peterson
Cover photo of table setting copyright © 2015 by Alicia Magnuson Photography/ Stocksy (#544499). All rights reserved.

Library of Congress Cataloging-in-Publication Data

Holleman, Heather E.
 Seated with Christ : living freely in a culture of comparison / Heather Holleman, PhD.
  pages cm
 Includes bibliographical references.
 ISBN 978-0-8024-1343-7
 1. Contentment—Religious aspects—Christianity. 2. Christianity and culture. 3. Social comparison. I. Title.
 BV4647.C7H65 2015
 234--dc23

2015017415

We hope you enjoy this book from Moody Publishers. Our goal is to provide high-quality, thought-provoking books and products that connect truth to your real needs and challenges. For more information on other books and products written and produced from a biblical perspective, go to www.moodypublishers.com or write to:

Moody Publishers
820 N. LaSalle Boulevard
Chicago, IL 60610

3 5 7 9 10 8 6 4 2

Printed in the United States of America

CONTENTS

Before You Begin . . .   9

Part One:
TAKE YOUR SEAT

1. Something Missing   13
2. A Single Verb   21
3. Where You Never Sat   37
4. Imagine the Round Table   49

Part Two:
SEATED AND SET FREE

5. From Appearance to Adoration   69
6. From Affluence to Access   87
7. From Achievement to Abiding   103

Part Three:
SEATED AND SURRENDERED

8. Four Hard but Great Questions   123

Part Four:
SEATED AND SENT

9. Available Living   145
10. Seated and Sent   165
11. Moment by Moment   179

Notes   187
Acknowledgments   191

For Ashley, Sarah, and Kate

BEFORE YOU BEGIN...

I can't stand me!

It's all I could think of when I got out of the hospital, wheeled through the front door of my home, and encountered the big mirror in our hallway. What I saw crushed me. I was no longer the tall, tanned, "most likely to succeed" good-looking girl heading to college. The mirror reflected a sad and swollen-faced quadriplegic, sitting frumpy and askew in an oversized wheelchair. And I hated it.

It didn't help that most of my girlfriends were heading out of state to top-notch universities, or flashing big engagement rings, or landing classy jobs in downtown high-rises. The cosmic dice had rolled in their favor, but I had lost out. My hands didn't work and my feet didn't walk, all because of a stupid dive and a broken neck.

Yet looking back, it was the best thing that could've happened to me.

From then on, I realized that comparing myself to others was seriously scary; it was emotional suicide. Besides, I knew I was in trouble when I'd measure myself up against a well-dressed store mannequin and come out on the losing end. Something had to change, and fast! My sense of security and significance simply had to come from somewhere, from Someone beyond me.

My diving accident made me see that "life on my feet" had been a frenetic cycle of comparing and competing with others. I was a Christian at the time, but suddenly a simple verse like Romans 12:2 seemed written for me: "Do not conform any longer to the pattern of this world, but be transformed by the renewing of your mind. Then you will be able to test and approve what God's will is—his good, pleasing and perfect will."

Humbled by my paralysis, I sought peace of mind and heart in a renewed understanding of my relationship with Jesus. My wheelchair became the prison that set me free—I learned how to grieve my losses in a healthy way and move forward in hope. I kept my eyes riveted on Jesus, and it made all the difference in the world. Over the years, I've come to see that Jesus is ecstasy beyond compare, and it is worth anything to be His friend.

I look back on that tall, tanned college-bound girl and wonder, *Does everyone caught in the culture of comparison need something drastic to initiate change? An awful injury or loss?* Thankfully, no! And this is why I am so heartened you are holding this remarkable book in your hands.

Seated with Christ is a wise and practical guide that will help you break free of feelings of failure and worthlessness. Heather Holleman has written a stellar work that plumbs the deepest recesses of our hearts, revealing ways in which we've all become tainted by our post-Christian culture. She has a Spirit-breathed ability to show you when you are promoting yourself . . . when you are trapped in people pleasing . . . and how you can rise above self-doubt and delusions.

So flip the page and get started. And please, don't plow through this book too quickly. Read its lessons prayerfully and act on their counsel intentionally. Get to the root of what ensnares you and take new, fresh steps toward freedom. Next to your Bible, this special book is your best companion in breaking free of our culture of comparison. Enjoy what it means to be seated with Christ. And the best news is, you don't have to break your neck to do it.

JONI EARECKSON TADA
Joni and Friends International Disability Center

PART ONE

—⟋⟍—

TAKE YOUR SEAT

———∿∿∿———

CHAPTER I

SOMETHING MISSING

I ache for something I cannot name.

—LAUREN SLATER, American psychologist

I was thirty-seven years old when I discovered a vital truth about Jesus.

A lightning bolt of realization hit me on a summer day in late July as I wondered over the phrase in Ephesians 2:6 that "God raised us up with Christ and seated us with him in the heavenly realms in Christ Jesus." I closed my eyes and began to think about my life.

I knew Jesus. I loved Jesus. I worshiped and served Him. I read my Bible, studied Christian concepts, kept a detailed prayer journal, shared my faith, met regularly with other Christians in church and in small group Bible studies, and worked for my community in various ways. I was the mom listening to Christian music in the kitchen, teaching Bible verses to my children, and rejoicing over what a great God I served. I loved my husband and our two beautiful elementary school–aged children. I blogged daily and wrote novels. Life often felt full and blessed.

But something was missing.

I did not know how to name it. Underneath the activity of my life ran a dark undercurrent of sin. I felt a subtle corrosion that something did not ring true about me. Something false, inauthentic, and impure governed my life. I felt like everything I did—all the activity, the writing, serving, speaking, studying—was about something other than Jesus. My life was more about *me* than Him. I was missing a theological truth that kept me in a prison of self-absorption.

I wanted importance and recognition.

I wanted love.

I wanted *something.*

When I read Ephesians 2:6, I thought about the word "seated." I kept repeating, "I'm seated with Christ." I imagined the security and sense of belonging that came with having a seat at the most important table in the universe with other Christians. How would that seated person live? What would it feel like to have a special place at God's royal table?

I was not living as one who had a seat at the table.

I lived as one *fighting* for a seat at the table.

It was as if God said to me, "Heather, you can stop fighting so hard. You already have a seat at the table. You are already there. Everything you want for yourself is already true about you in Christ. Now start living like a seated person."

—⁓—

Like me, many Christians miss this essential truth. We are missing a piece of a theological puzzle. We grasp that we are justified, forgiven, saved, sanctified, and redeemed. But *seated*? What does it mean? Why would the apostle Paul, in a historic moment when the church in Ephesus needed a precise understanding of the gospel, use this image and this verb instead of another?

I have spent decades trying to build up a theological vocabulary to understand who Jesus is and who I am in relation to Him. In all the years of learning in church settings and Christian communities, I never heard the word "seated" to tell me who I was.

Have you? Why have we missed this incredible word in Scripture? What I needed desperately to understand was this: I'm *seated*. I have a place at the greatest table the world has ever known. I belong. I'm in my seat, and I'm responding to specific instructions from the Lord about the "good works, which God prepared in advance" for me to do as promised at the end of Ephesians 2. The words in Ephesians 2:6 constitute a profound message of inclusion, identity, and calling.

Before that summer afternoon when I encountered Jesus afresh in the words of that letter to the Ephesians, I had served in vocational ministry for fifteen years. I was well-read, apparently strong in my faith, and fruitful in ministry.

COULD IT BE THAT I DID NOT REALLY *BELIEVE* I BELONGED, THAT I HAD A PLACE, AND THAT GOD HAD ACCEPTED ME AND INVITED ME TO SIT DOWN WITH HIM IN THE HEAVENLY REALMS?

I had even studied the psychology of emotion for five years for my doctorate in English literature and received theological and ministry training. But the dark corrosion persisted; I was still fighting hard for recognition and belonging. I knew something was wrong because I lived in shame on the one hand—tormented by failure, inferiority, and worthlessness—and narcissism on the other —exalting and promoting myself. I compared myself to others and felt either jealous or superior. I was consumed with evaluating myself in a sickened effort to prove my worth, find belonging, and receive acknowledgment from audiences both real and imagined.

What did this drive to earn my seat at the table produce? Poor boundaries, people-pleasing behaviors, constant self-evaluation, disconnection, fear of failure, self-doubt, controlling behaviors, over-eating, a sense of entitlement, delusions of fame, shame, a lack of vulnerability, a judgmental and critical attitude, and an easily offended spirit. Despite ten years of managing these symptoms in therapeutic and spiritual settings, I never quite got to the root of my immature and narcissistic behaviors. I could theorize why I acted certain ways, but I could not articulate with any satisfaction how to change.

So I confessed more, prayed harder to be controlled by the Holy Spirit, and read bestselling Christian self-help books. It seemed, to the outsider, like I was healing. I was even asked to share all my wisdom with others in leadership seminars.

Ironically, it was the same summer afternoon I began writing a talk on emotional maturity for Christian leaders in ministry that Jesus intervened and led me to Ephesians 2. Instead of delivering a presentation to leaders on healthy boundaries and emotionally mature behaviors, I changed the speech to get at the core of what drives unhealthy behaviors.

Quite clearly, managing these unwanted attitudes and behaviors is not the goal. We have to ask why they begin in the first place. I wondered then if all of my immaturity sprang from one leak in my theological understanding: Could it be that I did not really *believe* I belonged, that I had a place, and that God had accepted me and invited me to sit down with Him in the heavenly realms? Instead of pursuing the goal of emotional well-being, I wrote in my seminar notes that the real goal was one thing alone:

The goal is intimacy with Jesus.

I was indeed missing something, or rather, Someone. It was Jesus.

The goal is knowing Him and being with Him in the heavenly realms. Everything flows from this.

Without this goal of intimacy with Jesus, seated with Him in the heavenly realms, I live as one trying to earn a seat at whatever table happens to mean the most to me in any given season of life. Here are my tables, which currently appear (and have appeared) in various forms. Do we share the same struggles? What are your tables?

- The smart person's table (I will earn the PhD, publish prolifically, and earn a seat with the prestigious professors).
- The thin and beautiful table (I will work out harder, diet more, buy new clothes, and consider new beauty treatments).
- The good wife and mother table (I will keep a clean home, prepare delicious meals, plan creative and intellectually enriching activities, and then blog every day to show how great we're doing).
- The published authors' table (I will write book after book and one day be honored).
- The fruitful Christian missionary table (I will serve till exhaustion and lead others to faith so I can be somebody to my church).
- The wealthy family table (I will just earn more money).
- The famous table (I will be known for *something*, anything).

Ephesians 2:6 dispelled the darkness inside of me. Jesus says I'm *seated* with Him. I have a place at the table. I can stop fighting to prove my worth. Because I'm seated at the table, I'm invited to gaze at the Head, Jesus Christ, and allow Him to set me free from both self-exalting and self-condemning behaviors. I'm seated in a place that invites God's provision. I'm seated in a place that allows me to bear fruit for God's kingdom. I'm seated at a place where I belong—with Jesus and with other believers—and I won't ever have to battle loneliness, exclusion, or comparison again.

I felt like a warm balm had been applied to my heart.

I felt free from myself.

It seems so simple. It seems too easy and too good to be true.

But that's the gospel. That is exactly why Jesus Christ brings the best news the world will ever hear. A Savior has come to win a place for us and set us free.

We have a place at the table with Jesus.

SIT AND SAVOR

Read Ephesians 2:1–10.

1. When you read this passage in Ephesians, note the expression "alive with Christ" as opposed to "dead in transgressions." What do you think it means to be "alive with Christ"?

2. Paul repeats the expression "it is by grace you have been saved" twice in this passage. What does it mean to be saved by grace?

3. In what ways have you fought (or are still fighting) for recognition and belonging?

4. In what areas of your life are you tempted to compare yourself to others? When do you feel inferior? When do you feel superior?

5. Think of the table(s) where you're trying to earn a seat. What would having a seat there mean to you at this moment or season of your life?

CHAPTER 2

———— ୬୬ ————

A SINGLE VERB

And God raised us up with Christ and seated us
with him in the heavenly realms in Christ Jesus.
—EPHESIANS 2:6

It's autumn in Pennsylvania.

I walk around the campus of Penn State and crunch acorns and leaves with my boots. I'm tempted to jump into the leaves and roll around, but I'm nearly late for the writing course I teach. I smell the pumpkin-spice lattes of the college students who stream past me on their way to class. The midmorning sun filters through the burgundy and yellow trees, and the crisp air sends me diving into my bag for mittens.

I love the morning energy of the college campus: the jostling of books, the crinkle of term papers, and the rush of academic conversations continue to thrill me even after a decade of teaching. I'm smiling in anticipation of how I'll burst through the classroom door.

My students call me a "walking exclamation point," and I'm known for jumping up and down and clapping when a student uses a particularly clever verb. Most of my enthusiasm in teaching comes from my love of vivid verbs. When students use *grapple, fritter,* or *effervesce* correctly (my favorites), I'll even give extra points on that essay. The verb powers the whole sentence. With the verb, you create a mood and an image. "Look at these beautiful fall leaves outside," I'll say. "Tell me what you see!" If someone merely says, "The leaves are on the ground," I cringe and deflate before my students.

That weak verb, "are," means nothing to us. It shows us nothing and makes us feel nothing.

"Replace it with a vivid verb to create a mood and an image," I say, challenging them to go through the alphabet and find twenty-six other, more precise verbs. So they do: The leaves, in this case, *arrive, blanket, cavort, dance, effervesce, fritter, grapple with, hover, ignite, jostle, kamikaze, laugh, mourn, nod, obscure, pummel, query, ricochet, skip, tousle, usher, vacillate, wander, xanthate, yearn,* or *zip across* the ground. Yes, that's better.

I do love a great verb.

All semester, I invite students to employ amazing verbs. I tell them, "A great verb can change your life!"

I believe this as I read Ephesians 2:6. Here, Paul uses a great verb to change our lives. He provides a mood (how we feel) and an image (what we see) in one verb. Paul's declaration in Ephesians 2:6 that "God raised us up with Christ and *seated* us with him in the heavenly realms in Christ Jesus" (emphasis mine) offers us a new and proper way to think about ourselves. We aren't the center of our lives anymore; we're seated with Christ and other believers. The verb reorients us back to our true identities and, like any precise verb that empowers the whole sentence, we find our lives empowered afresh.

> WE'RE SEATED TOGETHER WITH A KINGDOM CONFERRED UPON US. WE ARE AT A ROYAL TABLE, SITTING DOWN WITH JESUS.

"Seated in Christ," translated from the Greek, means "to make us sit down together in Christ." The sense of togetherness within this verb matters to the Gentile audience for whom the letter to the Ephesians was primarily written. The idea that Jews and Gentiles would have a seat "together" in Christ might have seemed astonishing.

Equally astonishing is that Paul used the verb "seated" to an audience that would already know the special import of this word. A "seat" denoted an important place of honor. The root expression of this word in Greek also means "to confer a kingdom upon," so it's abundantly clear that Paul wants his readers to know just how important this concept is. In other words, *we are seated together in a royal setting, with a kingdom given to us.*

According to customs of the time, people around a table would sit, squat, or recline on the floor. If the event was important, ceremonious, or royal, attendants sat on seats. Even during great Jewish feasts, you as a guest would recline or squat unless you were part of the king's circle. Only then did you have an actual seat.[1]

Let's summarize: We're seated together with a kingdom conferred upon us. We are at a royal table, sitting down with Jesus.

When you think about being "seated," the verb also evokes a sense of rest and relaxation. It's a verb that feels safe. It's celebratory and peaceful. But Paul wrote this verb when he was perhaps the farthest away from safe, celebratory, and peaceful that a man could be. He wasn't physically at a royal table at all.

He was in a prison.

—⚬—

Paul's seat in prison, according to the Roman historian Gaius Sallustius Crispus, in his account of first-century Roman prisons, was "disgusting and horrible, by reason of the filth, darkness, and stench."[2] Scholars theorize that Paul was cold as he asks for a cloak, for example, in 2 Timothy 4:13. As we visualize this scene where Paul sits in the filth, darkness, putrid odors, and chill, I'm astonished that, despite his physical reality, in his spiritual reality, he was simultaneously seated in the heavenly realms with Christ. He knew—because of his position in Christ—that he could focus on a different kind of seat. Paul writes:

> Since, then, you have been raised with Christ, set your hearts on things above, where Christ is, seated at the right hand of God. Set your minds on things above, not on earthly things. For you died, and your life is now hidden with Christ in God. When Christ, who is your life, appears, then you also will appear with him in glory. (Colossians 3:1–4)

Paul, writing from that hard, cold, prison's ground, had his heart in a different place. His mind was not there. His life was elsewhere, in another seat. This seat with Christ captured Paul's heart and mind, and he chose, in even the direst circumstances, to celebrate how he had been "raised with Christ" and was now seated with Him in the heavenly realms.

Can you imagine knowing that you are seated at a royal table in the heavenly realms no matter what's actually happening in your physical experience? Paul did this, and so can I. And so can you. Do the implications take your breath away?

I began to research what made this experience of being "seated" so profound to Paul, and I found myself learning something even more beautiful. When you read in Ephesians 2 that we are raised "with" Christ and seated "in" Him, you must turn to Hebrews 10 and take a step back. You must ask yourself why it is so important that Jesus Christ Himself is "seated." Here is where I cover my face with my hands and close my eyes in wonder.

We know from Jewish law concerning the administration and service in the temple that Jewish priests were not allowed to *sit down*. They always stood. In fact, the tabernacle had no seats.[3] We read this incredible fact about Jesus:

> Day after day every priest stands and performs his religious duties; again and again he offers the same sacrifices, which can never take away sins. But when this priest [Jesus] had offered for all time one sacrifice for sins, he sat down at the right hand of God, . . . For by one sacrifice he has made perfect forever those who are being made holy. (Hebrews 10:11–12, 14)

The high priest *does not sit down*, yet here, Jesus, our High Priest forever, *sits down*. What can this mean? When I compare the verbs *stand* and *sit* in this passage, I begin to wonder what made the verb "sit" so remarkable to the audience. I found a great answer in a nineteenth-century sermon. On February 4, 1872, the British preacher Charles Spurgeon delivered a sermon on Hebrews 10 called, "The Only Atoning Priest." We read the following:

> The priests stood because there was work to do; still must they present their sacrifices; but our Lord sits down because there is no more sacrificial work to do; atonement is complete, he has finished his task. There were no seats in the tabernacle. Observe the Levitical descriptions and you will see that there were no resting-places for the priests in the holy place. Not only were none allowed to sit, but there was nothing whatever

to sit upon ... A priest never sat in the tabernacle, he was under a dispensation which did not afford rest, and was not intended to give it, a covenant of works which gives the soul no repose. Jesus sits in the holy of holies, and herein we see that his work is finished.[4]

Spurgeon's commentary on Hebrews 10 makes Ephesians 2:6 come alive even more. Jesus "sat down at the right hand of God" having finished, once and for all, the sacrifice for sin.

It is finished.

No sacrifice for sin—past, present, and future sin—is needed.

Jesus finished the work of the priests. He is the High Priest who takes away the sins of the world, and He invites me to take my seat in the heavenly realms beside Him.

Spurgeon does not end his sermon there; he says again that Jesus sat down, and "if I am a believer that is my posture, if you are a believer that is yours—you are to sit down ... Our justifying work is finished, finished by Christ. Sit down Christian, sit down and rest in thy Lord."[5]

P AUL TALKS ABOUT HOW WE HAVE *ALREADY BEEN SAVED* AND THAT WE HAVE *ALREADY BEEN MADE ALIVE WITH CHRIST.* THIS HAS ALREADY HAPPENED.

We can sit down. In fact, we *are* sitting down. We have been raised with Christ, who has "seated us" in the heavenly realms. As a writing instructor who specializes in grammar, I'm particularly delighted by the past tense statement that we have been seated.

It's a past tense verb.

It suggests something has already happened to us.

We've already been seated in the heavenly realms, yet here we remain in a physical body in a material world. Paul often put theological truths in the past tense in order to affirm the certainty of them happening at a future date, and he maintained the same simultaneity that I feel when I read this verb. It's a both now-and-not-yet kind of verb, just like when Jesus claims the "kingdom of God is in your midst" in Luke 17:21. We know that we will enter into heaven when we physically die, but there's also a sense that some part of the kingdom of heaven has already begun in us *right now.* The kingdom of God, like our seat in the heavenly realms, will come about in fullness as we enter heaven, but as believers, we are at this very moment part of God's kingdom and seated with Christ.

In Ephesians 2, most biblical scholars I've read believe that Paul's statement announces something true about us *in the present moment.* As I read Ephesians 2:6 in context, I find more evidence for this:

> As for you, you were dead in your transgressions and sins, . . . But because of his great love for us, God, who is rich in mercy, made us alive with Christ even when we were dead in transgressions—it is by grace you have been saved. And God raised us up with Christ and seated us with him in the heavenly realms in Christ Jesus, in order that in the coming ages he might show the incomparable riches of his grace, expressed in his kindness to us in Christ Jesus. For it is by grace you have been saved, through faith—and this is not from yourselves, it is the gift of God—not by works, so that no one can boast. For we are God's handiwork, created in Christ Jesus to do good works, which God prepared in advance for us to do. (vv. 1, 4–10)

Here, Paul talks about how we have *already been saved* and that we have *already been made alive with Christ*. This has already happened. So why would it not follow that his next statement reveals an equally accomplished reality? We *have been seated* in Christ in the heavenly realms. If this is something happening right now in the heavenly realms, and not at some future date, then what would it look like to add this verb to my arsenal of theological terms?

———∿∿———

I have a picture and a mood in my mind when I read the word "seated." I see myself called by a great king to my seat at the table. Can you see yourself called to your seat? In my imagination, it plays out like Arthurian legend and the famed Round Table.[6] I see a great round table, fit for the greatest knights of Camelot.

I know it's rather old-fashioned, and maybe the only image you have in your mind is Disney's 1963 animated classic *The Sword in the Stone* when you hear about King Arthur. Maybe you have vague memories of these Arthurian legends from history class when you studied the medieval period and this legendary fifth-century British king. I'm not sure what you see in your mind, but I'll share what I imagine.

I imagine King Arthur calling the knights of Camelot to the Round Table. If you remember, at the Round Table, nobody is inferior or superior to anyone else. King Arthur chose a round table for this very purpose: to settle disputes over superiority. Every knight was equal at the Round Table. In my mind, I see the knights take their seats. Each one has his own place, his own talents, and his own assignments. They sit battle ready, uniquely equipped, devoted to the kingdom, and interdependent.

Can you see them in your mind? Can you see the enormous

ancient table—rich and dark—that smells like the forest? Can you see the tall, sturdy chairs lined with red velvet and beset with jewels? Can you see the goblets and platters piled high with delicious food? As I let Jesus take my hand (and I'm in a sparkling gown, like Guinevere), I gather up my dress and take my seat. What about you? What are you wearing? What are you feeling? What are you doing?

When we see ourselves this way—as seated at the table and called to complete the tasks God assigns us—we stop working so hard for acceptance. We stop caring about prestige. We no longer need to make a name for ourselves, because we're completely absorbed in Christ and the kingdom. In this setting, we cease measuring ourselves against any other person. Why would we? We have our own seat, our own calling, and our own tasks. Plus, we're interdependent with one another, seated all together to make a holy dwelling place.

Scripture, after all, teaches about the *we* more than the *me*.

Think about John 11:52 where we read about how God's plan is to bring people "*together* and make them one," or how in 1 Corinthians 3:17 that "God's temple is sacred, and you *together* are that temple." Or what about Ephesians 2:22 and how we are "being built *together* to become a dwelling in which God lives by his Spirit"? Consider, finally, Philippians 1:27 and Paul's encouragement that we strive "*together* as one for the faith of the gospel" (emphasis added in above verses).

Together.

We have a seat together at the table. We are free to complete these tasks from a position of security, self-forgetfulness, and equality with others. We've already received the fullness of Christ and His righteousness. His power is available to accomplish all He calls us to do. Christ won a place for us, and we're seated in Him and with Him. We can stop fighting to win a spot.

That single verb—seated—has changed how I approach parenting, as well as teaching, writing, and ministry assignments. I've found that living as if I'm already seated at the table purifies my motivations in my work and ministry. I'm motivated by Christ's love and not a need to belong somewhere. I'm free from self-absorption and constant self-evaluation about whether I'm enough. I'm not fighting for a place. Whether I fail or succeed against some arbitrary standard no longer matters for my identity and my heart.

—⁓—

As I walk to class in a shower of falling golden leaves (they xanthate the ground; this means to make yellow, by the way), I experience a peacefulness and joy I can only describe as feeling *deeply seated* in Christ. I can identify several wonderful realities that stem from feeling seated in Christ:

- I'm doing what I'm made to do. Teaching and ministry are my specific good works, which God prepared in advance for me to do. I belong here. I'm confident in my tasks.
- I'm full of hope that God will shower innumerable good things into my hands. He's a gracious and loving Father. As the psalmist in Psalm 31:19 writes, "How abundant are the good things that you have stored up for those who fear you, that you bestow in the sight of all, on those who take refuge in you."
- I greet people with genuine love and encouragement as I see them as seated, too, in their own places, with

their own unique callings. I'm feeling neither inferior nor superior to them. Instead, I'm feeling interwoven with them, knit together as tightly as the stitches in these mittens.

- I gaze at the head, Jesus Christ, and fix my attention on Him in worship.

Secure. Hopeful. Loving. Worshiping. Something's changed within me because I finally believe I'm seated at the table.

—⟪⟫—

I'm at my writing desk as the late afternoon sun creeps behind the trees outside my window. I can smell the eucalyptus in a vase by my computer that combines with the scent of cinnamon and ginger from the harvest candle to my right. My older daughter, Sarah, sits to my left at a little desk with a craning lamp. She's working on prime factorization for math homework. She's humming. Her blonde hair falls across her cheek. It's one of those afternoons when a palpable peace descends on the home. The world feels right.

But it isn't. It's not right because that morning, my daughter's stomach hurt. She cried more than usual. She didn't want to go to school.

SHE TELLS ME HOW GIRLS HAVE SHUNNED HER FROM THE COOL GIRLS' TABLE. *SHE'S NOT COOL ENOUGH. SHE'S TOO AWKWARD.*

Sarah turns to me as I write my thoughts on Ephesians 2:6, and she quietly reports something she's been mulling over.

"Mom, I don't know where to sit in the lunchroom." She pauses. "I sit alone in the art room."

There it is. That wound reopens from my own middle school years.

There's a popular girls' table, and just like her mom wasn't, she's not invited to take a seat either. Her blue eyes look into mine, and I see fear, longing, and confusion. Loneliness. Rejection. Even though she's eleven years old, I take her onto my lap. She doesn't pull away. She tells me how girls have shunned her from the cool girls' table. *She's not cool enough. She's too awkward.*

"Do you know what I'm writing about?" I ask her.

"What?" she says, sitting there on my lap before the computer screen.

"I'm writing about how Jesus tells us we have a seat at His table in the heavenly realms. We have our own special seat with Him." I quote Ephesians 2:6 to her.

She nods. My voice cracks, and I pray she can't tell I'm damming up a river of tears from my own memories of middle school popular tables and dances and parties; I store up vivid pictures of all the places I never sat.

"Do you know what that means?"

She rests her head on my shoulder, waiting.

"It means you have a seat at the table. It's strange to imagine it—it's in your mind, but it's real even though you can't see it—that you are a royal princess at the greatest table in the world. It's not in the physical realm, but you're *there*. I mean, you're here, but you're also there."

I'm floundering. I'm praying.

Nothing. No response.

"I want you to remember that when you go to the lunchroom.

You are seated with Christ. Can you see it? Don't think about those popular girls. Don't think about them anymore. You have a seat at the best table already. You're wanted there. Jesus chose you for His table."

She turns her head up to the ceiling and closes her eyes. She's a little girl who needs to know she's seated at the table. She—and her mother, too—desperately need to believe it. I'm wiping away tears now. I better get it together before she slides off my lap and returns to her prime factorization.

"Yeah. I see it."

I can tell by the way she's smiling that she can. I see a sparkle in those eyes and a new hope rising up inside of her.

I'm no longer eleven years old, but when I enter a new place, I feel the same old insecurity. I wonder where I'm going to sit. I wonder where I belong. But now I repeat, "I'm seated with Christ." It's not some moment of wishful thinking or some New Age mantra; it's a declaration of *who I am* in the heavenly realms.

I'm secure and called to perform the good works that God prepared in advance for me to do. I therefore have no concern about my place anymore. I know where I am. I know I belong. When you greet me, I feel neither inferior nor superior. I feel honored and amazed at you as a beautiful creation who has a seat at the table with me.

And if you aren't yet a Christian, I invite you to join me at the greatest table the world has ever known.

SIT AND SAVOR

Read Hebrews 10:1–25.

1. What does it mean that Christ "sat down" in this passage? What does it mean for you personally?

2. As an imaginative exercise, describe your seat in the heavenly realms with as precise and vivid detail as possible. What do you see, hear, smell, taste, and feel? What are you wearing? What are you experiencing in your mind? If you'd rather draw a picture, you may.

3. Paul wrote that he was "seated in Christ" when he was sitting on a filthy prison floor. What are your life "seats" that seem difficult right now? Include health concerns, financial difficulties, location, relationships, career issues, and so on.

4. What changes would happen in your life if you believed you were "seated in the heavenly realms"? To help, complete the following sentences:

"Because I'm seated in Christ, I stop _____."

"Because I'm seated in Christ, I feel _____."

"Because I'm seated in Christ, I can _____."

5. What does it mean to you that we are seated both "in Christ" and "with Christ"?

CHAPTER 3

—ᨓᨓ—

WHERE YOU NEVER SAT

*A chair's function is not just to provide a place to sit; it is to provide
a medium for self-expression. Chairs are about status, for example.
Or signaling something about oneself. That's why the words chair,
seat and bench have found themselves used to describe high status
professions, from academia to Parliament to the law.[1]*

—EVAN DAVIS, British economist

M any people can recall—with precise detail—the places they never sat.

Whether it was the popular lunch table in seventh grade or the executive boardroom in adulthood, metaphorical tables with limited seating burn in our imagination. We live in the awareness of where we have never and will never sit: the thin and beautiful table, the great parent table, the perfect spouse table, the community leadership table, or the rich and famous table. As we long for a place at the table—of whatever kind—and can't seem to find one, we experience rejection, loneliness, and even inferiority.

I never sat at the popular table in seventh grade. I also never sat on the homecoming court in high school or college. I was never driven around the football field in a cherry red convertible, holding on to my crown and roses for dear life. The table of beauty and popularity offered no seats for me.

Perhaps another table? What about athletics? Instead of homecoming court or prom queen photographs, I would have a letter jacket and trophies displayed in my bedroom.

Reality: I can't kick a ball or run to save my life. Coaches hoped I could. In fact, due to my older sister's incredible talent for running (she made the varsity team freshman year, was on the state championship cross country team, and earned a college running scholarship; just this morning she ran ten miles before work), scouts came to my junior high school salivating over a potential genetic lottery win in me. They left the track, shaking their heads in disappointment as I heaved and panted after the first ten yards of the fifty-yard dash. It was a dramatic and shaming defeat for me as I clutched my chest for fear of heart failure and dehydration. I would never have a podium finish. I would never sit at a sports banquet.

I also can't add two-digit numbers in my head, so the math team seats weren't an option. I don't have an ounce of musicality within me, so the band and choir seats weren't happening. Where would I sit? Where was my *place*? I look back on those school years, and I wonder why I couldn't make a group of friends instead of living in constant fear and insecurity about my seat at the table.

I didn't know how to belong.

I was also—shall we say—a *peculiar* child. I walked around reciting the Gettysburg Address for fun in third grade and read grammar books to pass the time. Instead of connecting with others in school as I grew, I debated them to prove myself. I talked about Socrates and politics at lunch. I recited Keats's "Ode on a Grecian Urn" because I loved poetry so much. This was a sure path to social exclusion. I studied all the time and wrote speeches in my bedroom. True, I was a national debater and won awards for oratory, but this didn't win me any kind of deep friendships, except for two or three precious friends who persevered with me through my awkwardness and strange obsession with verbs. I felt lonely and disconnected most of the time, even if you saw me smiling in history class or laughing in the hallway after biology.

I did go to a prestigious and competitive college, but even then, I simply tried to find a seat at whatever table I thought the culture deemed most important. When I think of those years at the University of Virginia, I mostly remember struggle and shame and fear. I drank

I MISSED MY CHANCE. LIFE IS PASSING ME BY. I HAVE LIVED THE WRONG LIFE.

at fraternity parties, trying desperately to belong. I dieted and exercised to lose more and more weight. I exhausted myself in a quest to achieve the highest grades. I remember crying on my dorm room floor, wondering what Jesus meant when He said I might have abundant life. I knew this battle for success and belonging wasn't abundant life at all.

My late twenties and early thirties were dominated by my striving to earn my metaphorical seat in elite clubs: the great marriage table, the raising exceptional children table, the dream house table, the crafting my perfect career table, the publishing my books table, or, finally, the great Christian platform table. Sometimes, I would fantasize about the exclusive bestselling author table, or worse, I'd regret the past and feel like I was living the wrong life, like I missed my chance at greatness.

I missed my chance. Life is passing me by. I have lived the wrong life.

Part of my longing for that one seat at some exclusive table stems from the fact that I *have* sat in some extraordinary places. I had tea at the White House with Barbara Bush as a fifth grader and representative for her Reading Is Fundamental program. I sat in the winner's circle for oratory and writing competitions. I graduated with highest distinction from a prestigious university and then earned a PhD. Once, I was in a television commercial to promote a charity bike ride. I've been to an inaugural ball. I've met famous people. I visited Texas millionaires in their mansions, conversed with oil tycoons, and dined with company CEOs who are worth billions of dollars as part of donor events for a mission's organization. I've spent time with President George H. W. Bush in his vacation home because my debate team friend's father was part of the White House Press Corps, and she invited me along. I've won awards for teaching. I get attention for blogging and writing.

I just signed a book contract.

These are my seats that have given me momentary worth. You'd think those seats would satisfy, but still, they aren't enough. They don't make me feel included. They don't make me feel secure or deeply loved. Quite the contrary; they often leave me feeling temporarily superior and prideful. They

SOME RECALL A CHILDHOOD WHERE THE SIMPLE SEATS THEY DESPERATELY NEEDED DIDN'T EXIST FOR THEM.

also feed the addiction, like a street drug with diminishing returns.

Once I leave those seats in those settings, I'm still fighting for the next, more prestigious spot. I ruminate about every place I never sat, and I begin to fear for the places I will never sit.

—◊—

What are your seats? Can you list all those places that make you feel like you belong, that you're worthwhile, and that you've accomplished something great? Or, instead, do you think about where you never sat? When you think about the places you longed to sit, but never did, does something ache inside of you?

Some recall a childhood where the simple seats they desperately needed didn't exist for them: a father's lap, a seat at the dinner table with a real family, or just a neighborhood where they belonged. Some had everything in the way of family and money, but they still felt excluded from various groups. These children never felt quite comfortable in their own skin and wondered, even into adulthood, who they were and where they fit in.

Here's the summary: We weren't popular. We weren't the smartest. We didn't make the team. We wonder if we'll get married. Even as adults, we live in the past and grieve our losses: neglectful parents, unstable homes, and dysfunctional patterns forged by years of all kinds of abuse. Maybe we never cuddled up with a loving grand-

EITHER WE'RE PROTECTING THE SEAT WE HAVE OR WE'RE CLAMORING FOR THE SEAT WE NEVER HAD.

mother or sat at a dinner table where a parent delivered the Norman Rockwell steaming turkey, ready for carving by a loving and godly grandfather. We missed out; there's no bountiful table for us with crisp white linens and laughing relatives who love us. Instead, we might have been abused or abandoned in countless ways. Some of us live daily with injuries or health problems that have robbed us of our seat at the table of simply living pain free. Some of us sit at the table and only see the empty seats around us of loved ones who have died. Yes, we are grieving losses every day.

Our past shows us where we never sat, and our future features a parade of tables that we imagine will finally bring us life. We wonder what it must feel like to gather with the rich and famous. We want to belong in the club with the politically elite or the Christian influencers. We find ourselves driven to exhaustion as we fight for a place in our colleges, neighborhoods, workplaces, and even within our churches.

What are we really doing? Why are we working so hard? For what? For whom?

I just want to sit down.

But here's the terrible truth: Before I knew I was seated with Christ, I was still waiting for my seat, and I wasn't even sure how to name it. I kept thinking it was one thing, and then as soon as I took that seat, it was not enough. Those seats never delivered what they promised.

I was always waiting for an invitation at ever-elusive and increasingly exclusive tables. You might feel the same way.

Or maybe you do feel secure and confident somewhere: in your leadership role, clubs, dating relationships, marriage, parenting, community involvement, or personal projects. But what if any of these were taken away? What if the seat you love so much broke, like Baby Bear's seat did for Goldilocks? What happens when the younger woman takes your spot in ministry or at your company? What happens when the other girl gets the date or the acceptance to your dream school? What happens when you experience failure and rejection?

Either we're protecting the seat we have—like the popular girls in the school lunchroom claiming their turf—or we're clamoring for the seat we never had.

Both positions deeply disturb me.

Either way, we're battling a sickening kind of self-obsession that keeps us comparing ourselves to others. We wonder where we belong, whether we're liked, and if we would ever "arrive."

We're measuring our lives against everyone else's. Many of us wonder, with every status update, picture, tweet, and blog, if we're worthy. Are we liked enough on Facebook, retweeted on Twitter, and repinned on Pinterest? Do we have platform and clout? We measure our blog traffic like doctors assessing vital signs for health. We fantasize about going viral or about trending on Twitter. Then, we'll belong. Then, we'll finally have a seat at the table we've been waiting for all our lives.

W HEN AS CHRISTIANS WE FIND OURSELVES MORE AND MORE TRAPPED IN THE RHETORIC OF PLATFORM AND PERSONAL MINISTRY IMPACT, WE NEED A LADDER OUT OF THE FRAY.

⁓〰⁓

Our fight for a seat at the table represents our desire for belonging and importance, but it also signifies all the ways we put ourselves at the center of our experience. We want the throne, not the round table. When we don't understand our seat in the heavenly realms, we battle for success and recognition. We clamor for fame.

When as Christians we find ourselves more and more trapped in the rhetoric of platform and personal ministry impact, we need a ladder out of the fray. As we better understand the implications of "seated," we can better discern the dangerous trend in both secular and Christian culture to exalt the self.

And it begins early.

In a study conducted at the University of California, fame was found to be "the major aspiration of children from ten to twelve years of age."[2] And over half of the eighteen- to twenty-five year olds surveyed in a Pew Research Center poll claimed that being famous was their generation's most important or second-most-important life goal; 81 percent said the same about being rich.[3] This generation's mantra includes what many of us fear our own children might express: I want to go viral. I want to trend on Twitter. I want to be the next American Idol. I want to be worshiped. The California study concluded, "young adults have, over the decades, become more focused on self, unrealistically ambitious, and oriented toward material success—all individualistic values that resonate with the value of fame."[4] Indeed, the researchers used this study to confirm that "fame [is] the number one cultural value" today.[5]

Perhaps more than any other time in history, we obsess over ourselves and whether or not people are thinking about us. With immediate feedback and ranking on social media sites, we know at any given time how we measure up against other people. At the end of the day, we find ourselves feeling inferior, or—equally problematic—superior. In our quest to belong somewhere, to claim our seat at the table, we've cultivated an acute self-consciousness that keeps us preoccupied with ourselves. We know we're being watched. And we're watching others all day long, too, through YouTube, Tumblr, Vine, Instagram, Twitter, Pinterest, and, most predominantly, Facebook (900 million monthly users to date).[6]

A Stanford researcher asked if Facebook was making us sad. In the January 2011 issue of *Personality and Social Psychology Bulletin*, Alex Jordan drew on a series of studies examining how college students evaluate moods, both their own and those of their peers. Not surprisingly, Jordan found that Facebook makes us feel dejected. As we see posts and pictures of everyone else's artificially perfect lives, we overestimate their happiness, and by comparing ourselves to them, find ourselves miserable.[7]

Interestingly, other research showed that we feel so disconnected after viewing Facebook that we try to solve this problem by looking at *more* Facebook to generate an illusion of connectedness.[8]

In other words, we're trapped in a prison of comparison. We're caught in an addictive feedback loop that we can't exit. We're killing ourselves to buy new shoes, purses, cars, houses, or land a better job just to prove our worth on social media. We push our children into impossible schedules of activities to ensure their belonging in some imaginary club that we certify through posts about their dance recitals, lacrosse games, and skiing lessons. We make elaborate dinners to photograph as evidence of our significance.

On a good day, we feel better than others. Smug and confident, we prance around, touting our own successes with pithy tweets, Photoshopped pictures, and self-congratulatory status updates. On these days, we self-promote and grab all the glory for ourselves that we can. We announce, "100 likes on my photo!" or "I have 15 retweets! People love me!"

BOTH SUPERIORITY AND INFERIORITY ARE DIFFERENT SIDES OF THE SAME COIN.

That's me: I'm either hiding in shame and inferiority or showcasing myself in a kind of narcissistic display. As I look at biblical narratives, I discover that Satan wants us to obsess over ourselves. He either tempts us to want to be like God, or he sends us into hiding with the tormenting sense of inferiority that psychologists call shame.

Psychologist Silvan Tomkins explains that shame is ultimately a fear of rejection or abandonment. It is the overwhelming belief that we are insufficient and that others see us as being so. Tomkins called shame an emotion of "relatively high toxicity." Shame, he writes, "strikes deepest into the heart of man . . . it is felt as a sickness of the soul which leaves man naked, defeated, alienated, and lacking in dignity."[9]

Both ways of relating—either narcissism (the state of loving and admiring oneself) or shame (feeling one is an unworthy person)—are symptoms of an excessive focus on self. Both superiority and inferiority are different sides of the same coin. They both reflect a narcissistic temperament that keeps us imprisoned to self-evaluation, self-consciousness, and self-absorption. As a result, we live isolated lives, consumed with how we compare to others.

A NEW LIGHT DAWNS: THE SEAT YOU'VE BEEN LONGING FOR ALL YOUR LIFE IS HERE AT LAST.

So we just keep fighting for a spot. We want the "good life," and we want to make sure everyone else knows we have it.

As I think about what the world designates as "the good life," I'm convinced that Satan's plan is to lure us away from realizing our seat with Christ by offering counterfeit seats that call to us with irresistible siren songs. For some, the song we hear comes in the form of Christian celebrity culture: bestsellers, talk-show interviews, speaking invitations, and ministry metrics. The seat in this case is adorned in numbers, money, and trends. If you're talked about, you're seated. If you have speaking engagements, you're seated. If you get a book deal, you're seated. If you win awards, you're seated.

Or maybe you're reading this, and you don't hear that song, but you hear the one about community service. If you're serving, involved in social justice, exhausted by local service projects or even abroad, well then, you're seated at the table. Or you hear the song about home ownership, getting your children into a great college, retirement, or vacations. The seated life, then, means something else entirely. It's about security. Maybe you're thinking about graduate school acceptances, job offers, or romantic proposals. Maybe being "seated" means living in the right city, with the right kind of home décor, and the right kind of coffeemaker.

Maybe being seated means you have the thinnest thighs or the clearest skin. Maybe you're a student reading this and you believe that a sorority bid, a date to the formal, or a simple invitation to have dinner in the dining hall with friends would mean you finally have a seat.

What is the seat you eye as the answer to the questions, "What is the good life? What constitutes success? What will make me happy?" What if the answer was something as simple as being seated with Christ in the heavenly realms? The places you've never sat and the siren song seats that lure you dissolve into the shadows. A new light dawns: The seat you've been longing for all your life is here at last.

In this seat in the heavenly realms with Jesus, you can be free from self-consciousness, from comparing yourself to others, and from being so preoccupied with whether you have a seat at the table that you're missing the incredible life in Christ that could be yours. I write to you as one healed of shame, narcissism, and self-promotion. I write to you as one healed of loneliness and jealousy.

I write to you as one so transformed by taking my seat in the heavenly realms that those dearest to me—those who know me best—have said, "What has happened to you, Heather? What has changed in you? You are finally free."

I am finally free.

SIT AND SAVOR

———✲———

Read Psalm 119:37.

1. What memories do you have of being excluded from certain "tables" (groups, clubs, events, etc.)?

2. What were the "best seats" you've ever had in your life?

3. When did you last feel like you really belonged to a community? What was that like for you? Describe how this community functioned.

4. What seats do people imagine will bring them the "good life"? What makes these seats, as the psalmist writes in Psalm 119:37, "worthless things"?

5. Why do you think fame and wealth have become the most important cultural values to young people? What about our culture feeds this trend?

—⚜—

CHAPTER 4

IMAGINE THE ROUND TABLE

I am a Knight of the Round Table
and well known in Arthur's realm.

— Knight Palamides in Sir Thomas Malory's
King Arthur and the Knights of the Round Table

One summer, I found myself absorbed in the BBC production of *Merlin*, the British fantasy-adventure series based on the Arthurian legend.

A neighbor recommended it to our family as a perfect series to enjoy. This program imagines the characters in the classic Arthurian tales as much younger than we usually regard them. We meet Merlin as a young warlock, and a young Arthur who has yet to assume the throne. The *Merlin* adventures captivated our whole family that summer. We couldn't wait to clear the dinner table, wash the dishes, and race to the television to watch Colin Morgan as Merlin interacting with the arrogant but adorable Arthur played by Bradley James. Who wouldn't love the dragon, the young wizard, and the budding romance between Arthur and Guinevere?

Certain aspects of Arthurian legend I remembered from my childhood; I knew about the sword and the stone whereby Arthur proves his right to be the king of Camelot. Most important,

I knew of the famous Knights of the Round Table, which came to represent the whole chivalric order of Camelot. I knew that it was a round table, with no head, to symbolize that no knight was more important than another. Instead of competing for a special seat, each knight could focus on the good of Camelot.

I had no idea that this fabled table, so deeply embedded in British folklore, would forever change how I saw myself.

In the third season of this series, the young King Arthur calls his men (and a woman, and an elderly man) to sit at a table. Arthur pulls the dusty covering off of an old, round table. As the background music plays, you see the king considering this table. After a few moments, he says to his companions, "Here, come and join me." Slowly, the audience watches as Lancelot, Gawain, and the other men gather. Arthur also takes Guinevere by the hand to help her to a seat at this old table.

Arthur says, "This table belonged to the ancient kings of Camelot. A round table afforded no one man more importance than any other. They believed in equality in all things, so it seems fitting that we revive this tradition now. Without each of you, we would not be here." He then explains part of his mission to defend Camelot, and then asks, "Are there any around this table who will join me?"

Each of his companions—young, old, male, female, rich, poor, educated, and unschooled—pledge their loyalty to Arthur, who says, "I want to thank you all for staying loyal to me in Camelot's hour of need. I'll do something that my father would approve of."

Now each knight kneels before Arthur, and he touches each shoulder with his sword. "Arise Sir Lancelot, Knight of Camelot," he says with authority. Arthur moves down the line of knights until each man receives that special anointing as a Knight of Camelot.

Finally, Arthur says, "Tomorrow when you fight, you can stand proud, knowing you are members of the most noble army the world has ever known."[1]

I'm in my pajamas, stuffing popcorn into my mouth and sipping tart lemonade, flanked by my daughters, and I find myself overcome with emotion. It was this scene, this Round Table, that came to my mind when I read Ephesians 2:6. It was this scene that my daughter and I talked about in the weeks after her middle-school lunchroom rejection from the popular girls' table.

This Round Table gave me the image I needed. We can observe several things about the Knights of Camelot.

Both historically and in the BBC's reimagining of Arthurian legend, the Knights of Camelot are consumed with devotion to the king and kingdom. They pledge their very lives to the king. In Galatians 2:20 Paul proclaims, "I have been crucified with Christ and I no longer live, but Christ lives in me. The life I now live in the body, I live by faith in the Son of God, who loved me and gave himself for me."

I thought of that kind of devotion. A crucified-self kind of devotion. An I-no-longer-live kind of devotion. A knight-to-his-king kind of devotion. In light of this incredible kingdom calling and devotion, my jealous squabbles and longing for earthly importance seemed silly and distracting.

The Knights of Camelot sit at the Round Table battle-ready, uniquely equipped, uniquely contributing, and bold and stout-hearted as lions. I watched them, and I thought of mighty lions. I thought

SOMETHING ABOUT THE ROUND TABLE IN ARTHURIAN LEGEND PROVIDED A WAY TO SEE MYSELF AS SEATED IN CHRIST.

of the times I read about lions in Scripture. I remembered Proverbs 30:30 and the description of the lion that's "mighty among beasts, who retreats before nothing." Yes, a Knight of Camelot is mighty; he's impressive in power and in strength. He retreats before nothing. I found myself sitting taller in my seat. I flexed a few muscles. I tilted my chin up and squared my shoulders. I felt strong and noble.

The Round Table "afforded no one man more importance than anyone else." The idea that no person mattered more than another, that no person was more valuable, more precious or more acknowledged, that no person was fighting for a place anymore filled my heart with a strange new peace. I never imagined myself at a round table with a seat for us all.

Something about the Round Table in Arthurian legend provided a way to see myself as seated in Christ. The parallel to Christ and His kingdom makes so much sense. Every time I spoke on being seated in Christ in the following months, I used the film clip of King Arthur calling the knights to the table to let audiences experience the same images I saw that night. That night, I thought of myself as "part of the most noble army the world has ever known." I smiled and shook my head at the simplicity of it. In my mind, I said this to my weary soul:

I have a place. I have a mission. I have a King I have devoted my life to. I'm uniquely called, uniquely contributing, and uniquely loved just like everyone else at the table. I can cease comparing myself to others. Nobody's inferior. Nobody's superior. We're on a mission together, and we're too busy serving a great King to bother with comparison and self-consciousness.

I finally belonged at the table.

—⁂—

As I thought about this image of interconnectedness and studied passages in the Bible that help me understand my identity in Christ, I realized the phenomenon that we are *together* a holy dwelling place, and *together* is something precious to Jesus. Doesn't Jesus pray for our unity in John 17? Doesn't Paul in Galatians 3 talk about how in Christ there are no slaves or free man, male or female, Gentile or Jew, but that we "are all one in Christ Jesus"? And what about the words in Romans 2:11 that "God does not show favoritism"? The original Greek verb for "seated," if you remember, is the sense of "sitting down all together."

The implications of sitting down together like this—interconnected and equal—are profound, not just for our loneliness, but for our realization of biblical community. Our seats in Christ destroy any possibility of racism, sexism, classism, and ageism. We do not judge one another at this table. We do not believe we are inferior or superior, no matter what our skin color, age, country of origin, possessions, or education.

That Christian woman who annoys you? She's seated at this table. The homeless brother in Christ you'd rather avoid? He's seated at this table. What about those Christians who do things you don't feel comfortable with for whatever reason? They are right here, too. The Christians who worship in a different denomination? I see them at the table. Those from a different political party? There. What about the mentally ill? What about prisoners? What about the drug addicts living day to day to accept their new life in Christ? What about any person you might discriminate against for any reason at all?

It doesn't matter at this table. No one is inferior. No one is superior.

In fact, ask yourself how someone gets a seat at this table.

How did you get a seat? Is it because of your good, socially acceptable behavior? No.

Answer: Jesus gives it to you. For free. To you. For no reason other than that He bought it for you at the price of His own precious blood. If you think you don't belong at this table for whatever reason—sexual sin, crime, a damaged past, addictions, just not special enough—you are 100 percent wrong.

We don't sit down because of who we are or what we've done or not done.

We sit down because Jesus offers us a seat. Jesus is seated because He finished the work. He made a final sacrifice for our sin, once and for all.

But before you can fully accept others in their seats, you need to visualize your own. In my mind, it's the grandest table—maybe a rich maple. I'm sitting in a large, comfortable chair, perhaps lined in red velvet. Some days, I'm wearing a beautiful gown. Other days, I'm lacing up my boots to go out on the mission with God. On all days, I repeat, "I'm seated with Christ," and then I recall Ephesians 2:10 where God says I'm "created in Christ Jesus to do good works, which God prepared in advance for [me] to do."

When you read Arthurian legend, in particular Sir Thomas Malory's version, you might be delighted to note that whenever a man introduces himself, he often says, "I'm a Knight of the Round Table and well-known in Arthur's realm."[2] The man repeated his identity to others over and over again. He's in service to the king and "well-known." He isn't clamoring for recognition or a seat at the table. He's *already known*.

So I say, "I'm Heather. I'm seated with Christ in the heavenly realms and well-known by Him!"

As I look through the Bible, a simple word study of *table, seat,* or *seated* provides outstanding images to carry in my mind as I read Ephesians 2:6. I'm moved to tears, for example, when I see King David searching for one of Saul's descendants to whom he might show favor. He finds

THIS ROYAL TABLE HAS A SPOT FOR US. HE PREPARES THIS TABLE FOR US.

Mephibosheth, the son of his beloved friend Jonathan and Saul's grandson. In 2 Samuel 9:3 we're told that Mephibosheth was "lame in both feet."

The king wanted to show kindness to this man—this unsightly, unproductive man—because of his covenant relationship to Jonathan who has died by this point in the narrative. When David finds Mephibosheth in verse 7 of this account, he says, "Don't be afraid, . . . for I will surely show you kindness for the sake of your father Jonathan. I will restore to you all the land that belonged to your grandfather Saul, and you will always eat at my table." Later, in verse 11, we're told that Mephibosheth would sit at this royal table "like one of the king's sons."

Think about it: a man who could have been sentenced to death as an enemy of the kingdom receives a royal invitation to a table he does not deserve. Remember that this man can contribute nothing. Additionally, as if this seat weren't enough, King David gives a fortune to Mephibosheth in land and servants; in fact, he gives back to Mephibosheth Saul's property in terms of land, servants, livestock, and crops. What an overwhelming picture of someone called by a great king to a table to take a place of royalty! We know that Mephibosheth receives this invitation wholeheartedly and lives in adoration and devotion to the king. We're even told that this otherwise nobody of a man later has a son. He has a place. He has a family. He belongs. He's important to the kingdom.

He sits at the king's table.

We are at the King's table, where the Ancient of Days sits (Daniel 7:9), where our great King is "seated at the right hand of the mighty God" (Luke 22:69). This royal table has a spot for us. He prepares this table for us; He spreads it out in the presence of our enemies (Psalm 23:5) and He does so in what we perceive as the wasteland and wilderness of our lives (Psalm 78:19).

There's a royal table, and we can take our seats right this very moment.

—⁓—

Are you seated yet? You can sit back in your chair and enjoy Jesus, and by extension, enjoy your beautiful and God-ordained life. When I visualize myself as at the table, seated in my spot with the life God has planned for me with the accompanying good works, blessings, and circumstances (even if these include suffering or loss), I stop comparing myself. I stop living in isolation and fear. I need not feel insecure, or, on the flip side, superior and boastful. I realize that God has exact instructions for me—part of the good works prepared for *me*—and other people have exact instructions for *their* lives. God has blessings prepared for them, and God has blessings prepared for me.

For example, before I realized I was seated in Christ, every woman's gain felt like my loss. If a woman was thinner, wealthier, or more accomplished, I would mope around as I thought about all the things I wished were different about my life. If I visited a beautifully decorated home, you can bet that night I complained to my husband about ours. If someone else's children excelled in school, I came home and pushed my children more to succeed. If that woman shared good news about a new car, a new vacation home, or a new opportunity, I silently seethed with jealousy.

Nothing ever felt like enough. I couldn't find contentment. I identified with the older brother in the story of the prodigal son. Do you remember that story Jesus tells in Luke 15? I invite you to read it again through the lens of that older brother being "seated in Christ."

To summarize, a father has two sons. The younger brother asks for his share of the estate and squanders all that wealth in foolish and wild living. After wallowing in poverty, he finally comes to his senses and decides he will go back and plead for his father's forgiveness in hopes that maybe he'll find work as a servant.

The father, so filled with compassion as he sees his son coming from afar, says to his servants, "Quick! Bring the best robe and put it on him. Put a ring on his finger and sandals on his feet. Bring the fattened calf and kill it. Let's have a feast and celebrate. For this son of mine was dead and is alive again; he was lost and is found" (vv. 22–24).

At this point, you might imagine that the older brother would share his father's joy. But in the text we read this:

> Meanwhile, the older son was in the field. When he came near the house, he heard music and dancing. So he called one of the servants and asked him what was going on. "Your brother has come," he replied, "and your father has killed the fattened calf because he has him back safe and sound."
>
> The older brother became angry and refused to go in. So his father went out and pleaded with him. But he answered his father, "Look! All these years I've been slaving for you and never disobeyed your orders. Yet you never gave me even a young goat so I could celebrate with my friends. But when this son

of yours who has squandered your property with prostitutes comes home, you kill the fattened calf for him!"

"My son," the father said, "you are always with me, and everything I have is yours. But we had to celebrate and be glad, because this brother of yours was dead and is alive again; he was lost and is found." (Luke 15:25–32)

The older brother forgot that he was seated. The father says, "You are always with me, and everything I have is yours." The older brother had the party *every day*. He could enjoy his father *every day*. Perhaps if the older brother had known that reality, he could indeed celebrate and rejoice about the ways the father blesses others.

When we are seated in Christ, we know that we are with God and everything He has is ours. Therefore, we celebrate the lavish love that Jesus pours out on others. It does not take away from the lavish love we experience of Jesus ourselves.

Before I fully grasped the implications of being seated in Christ that summer afternoon, I was the older brother. To confess, I compiled a mental list of all the women I resented out of jealousy. I listed all the ways I never rejoiced with a woman in her success because I thought it diminished my own. I listed it all out—every bitter, jealous thought—and then realized something.

That woman is seated in Christ. That sister in Christ is seated in her own spot, in her own life. If Jesus wants to bless her with beautiful clothes, obedient children, glamorous vacations, and prestigious awards, then that's part of her seat in Christ. That's what God has appointed for her. I can rejoice with her for her seat in Christ in the heavenly realms, because this is her journey, her life, and her blessings doled out by a loving heavenly Father.

I have my own journey, my own life, and my own blessings specifically planned and given to me. As do you. I'm seated in Christ, so if God plans something extraordinary for me to do, that's part of my seat. No matter what, I have all of Jesus at all times.

I have all of Jesus at all times.

—⁓—

Years ago, I found a quote in a novel by Lorrie Moore as I browsed books in the public library. It's from the museum guide of the Hayden Planetarium. The guidebook states, "All seats provide equal viewing of the universe."[3] I read it out loud, and the truth of it seemed to catch in my throat. I emailed the media director at Hayden Planetarium to learn more about this quote. I corresponded with a woman who said that the planetarium is designed so that no matter where you sit, you see the exact same images. No matter where you sit, you won't miss any part of the show.

No matter where you sit, you won't miss anything. I almost burst into tears.

I imagined all the children on field trips racing into the planetarium auditorium as the doors swing open. I imagine them all fighting for the best seats in an arena that has no best seats. I imagine the calm voice of the tour guide saying, "Children, all seats provide equal viewing of the universe."

As I read about the planetarium, it seemed that some great voice of wisdom gently whispered in my ear. I

ALL SEATS ARE EQUAL. YOU CAN STOP FIGHTING FOR A SPECIAL SEAT. *ALL* THE SEATS ARE SPECIAL SEATS.

realized that in every circumstance, I have full access to everything I need. I turned to my daughter and read it to her.

"Do you know what that means?" I asked. "It means that no matter where you are, you have an *equal chance* to perceive the beauty of God. All seats are equal. You can stop fighting for a special seat. Your seat *is* the special seat. *All* the seats are the special seats."

When I want to trade seats to find a better view, I'm going to sit tight and realize my equal chance to see—right where I am—the beautiful things God wants to show me. I'm seated in Christ, and it's a beautiful view. All seats provide equal love, equal access, equal blessing. I think Paul acutely experienced this reality as he wrote from the disgusting prison seat. He was beaten, hungry, exhausted, and poor. He was humiliated, cold, and alone. Yet, he was seated in Christ in the heavenly realms, and from that view of the universe, he knew the "secret of being content in any and every situation" (Philippians 4:12).

Two women I once envied invited me out to dinner. Sure enough, before I even took my first sip of coffee, one told me her plans for a lavish vacation including a chartered boat to a remote island. She talked about the gourmet dinners she'd enjoy with her well-dressed, popular children.

Guess how I responded?

I found myself *joyously laughing* with her about all the incredible experiences she would have with this amazing family God had given her. I talked about all the seafood and steaks she'd enjoy. I visualized us seated together in Christ in the heavenly realms. I knew that God had chosen to pour some wonderful things into my friend's life, and I felt—for the first time in my life—freedom from jealousy or comparison.

When it was my turn to share about our glamorous plans for vacation, I talked about staying home, writing, walking in the woods, and baking. *All seats provide equal viewing of the universe.* My simple vacation could be just as filled with the glory of God as hers. But it went deeper than that; I didn't even want to compare. It seemed silly, like someone comparing avocados to coffee. Why would I? It makes no sense.

As I sat there at the restaurant and imagined myself seated with Christ, I didn't worry about feeling excluded, inferior, or superior. I'm seated with Christ at my special place in the heavenly realms. Therefore, I imagine my seat. I say in my mind, "I'm seated with Christ in the heavenly realms. I belong. I'm included. I'm totally secure. Now how can I bless these people?"

Whenever I feel insecure in any setting, in fact, I think about blessing others. If I worry about teaching or mentoring or even cooking dinner, I imagine my seat and repeat in prayer, "I'm seated with Christ and there are all sorts of good works God has prepared in advance for me to do. I'm available to do them, so Jesus, please empower me right now to teach this lesson, mentor this woman, or cook this meal to bless others."

In large ways and small ways, I know I'm seated with Christ: When I'm vacuuming and cleaning toilets, I'm seated with Christ at a royal table. When I'm on stage giving a speech to a thousand people, I'm seated with Christ and no more important than when I'm cleaning the bathroom at home. When I'm raising my children, I'm seated with Christ. He chose these children for me to raise, and I'm the perfect mother for them. My children, too,

> BECAUSE YOU'RE SEATED IN CHRIST AT YOUR OWN SEAT, THIS DAY WILL LOOK NOTHING LIKE YOUR BEST FRIEND'S, YOUR COWORKER'S, OR YOUR NEIGHBOR'S.

are seated with Christ, and I can cease fretting about the lives God has planned for them.

Finally, when I feel frantic, like I'm not doing enough, or doing too much, I remember that I'm seated with Christ. Jesus ordered His day around the Father's *exact* instructions. No more, no less. Jesus says yes to what He's supposed to say yes to. He declines what He must decline. He travels here and there under divine order.

As you think about your special seat, and the tasks before you today, recall John 14:31 where Jesus says, "I love the Father and do exactly what my Father has commanded me." We can do exactly what God commands. Not what my culture says I must do, not what magazines or Pinterest tell me I must do, not what Christian bloggers tell me I must do, but what the Father has commanded me to do.

When I look more closely at Jesus' life in the Gospel accounts, I note how He knows when to stop talking and when to speak. He knows when to get up and leave, and He knows when to stay. He does *exactly* what He's supposed to do. He doesn't consider what everyone else does. He does what He's supposed to do. He's following a different set of instructions.

Just a few verses earlier, we read that we can do exactly what Jesus instructs because the Holy Spirit teaches us "all things" and "remind[s]" us of everything we've been taught (John 14:26). If the Holy Spirit teaches us all things, can't we ask God for specific instructions for our day? We pray and ask, and then we order our day *exactly*.

Because you're seated in Christ at your own seat, this day will look nothing like your best friend's, your coworker's, your neighbor's, or anyone else's pictures on social media.

What will it look like? It will look *exactly as it's supposed to look* because you're seated with Christ in the heavenly realms. You have your own calling today. You have your own "good works that God has prepared in advance" for you to do.

Recently, I sat in the bedroom, just staring at Philippians 2:13. Here, Paul writes that God works in me to "will and to act in order to fulfill his good purpose." I learned it means this: God gives you the desire and the ability to accomplish His plans for you.

God gives me the desire and the ability to accomplish His plans for me.

I don't need to worry about any other seat at this table in the heavenly realms. I just sit in my seat and understand that God is working in me to live the life He has planned for me.

As Theodore Roosevelt said, "Comparison is the thief of joy." I heard this quote years ago, but I didn't know how to stop comparing myself to others. Now I can. I can because I imagine, on a daily basis, that I'm seated with Christ in the heavenly realms.

Imagine it: You're a Knight at the Round Table. We're about to move into a brand-new kind of living. Get ready to start living the life God has planned. You just need to take your seat and let the show begin. But repeat after me: *I am seated with Christ in the heavenly realms.*

Now that you know this to be true, we can discuss how seated people live. I was an expert in how unseated people live—the comparison, the fixation on beauty, the obsession with wealth, and struggle for achievement. In fact, my counselor, Dr. Gregory Hocott, provided an apparatus for me to understand the predictable battle of those who misunderstand their identity in Christ when I came to him for help with depression and anxiety in my early twenties.

The stresses of postpartum depression and pregnancy weight gain coupled with a thyroid disorder that left me looking like a balding blowfish with cracked skin; my husband's transition to a full-time ministry position (he'd leave a lucrative job and we'd rely on ministry donors for our salary and expenses); and working on the dissertation for my PhD with a new baby (a recipe for disaster) disabled everything I valued about myself: a thin and young body, a wealthy lifestyle with all the accoutrements of affluence, and status as a university professor.

Dr. Hocott said it was a special grace of God that He was removing all my possible coping mechanisms and all of my "false selves" that ultimately kept me from understanding my position as seated in Christ. He said that I was suffering because I had built my life around the "Three As: Appearance, Affluence, and Achievement."[4]

In the following chapters, you'll see how a seated person moves even more deeply into the reality of her identity in Christ. Instead of the three As—Appearance, Affluence, and Achievement—of the unseated life, you can experience another set of As: Adoration, Access, and Abiding. Just wait; you're going to love the seated life.

SIT AND SAVOR

—∿∿—

Read the account of King David and Mephibosheth in 2 Samuel 9 and the parable of the prodigal son in Luke 15.

1. Imagine you are both Mephibosheth and the prodigal son. What might make it difficult to receive such mercy and love?

2. Imagine you are the older brother in the Luke passage. Make a list of the bitter, jealous thoughts that have formed in your heart due to comparison. How does being "seated in Christ" help soothe the jealous feelings?

3. Imagine you are seated at a table with all the people that you find difficult to love and accept. Be very honest with yourself about your personal prejudices against others. Do you discriminate against others because of their race, possessions, education, abilities, or age? How does being seated in Christ change these feelings?

4. List your greatest insecurities. Now imagine you are seated in Christ as you enter a new situation. What changes in your mind as you think about your seat in the heavenly realms?

5. Imagine your particular life story, and think about where you live and work. Can you give an example of how "all seats provide equal viewing of the universe"? Where have you experienced the beauty and glory of God right where you are?

PART TWO

—ɯ—

SEATED AND SET FREE

—✸—

CHAPTER 5

FROM APPEARANCE TO ADORATION

Those who look to him are radiant;
their faces are never covered with shame.

—KING DAVID, PSALM 34:5

Worship your body and beauty and sexual allure and
you will always feel ugly. And when time and age start
showing, you will die a million deaths.

—DAVID FOSTER WALLACE

When I attended the University of Virginia, I, like most other girls my age, obsessed over my appearance.

I longed for a seat with the beautiful people. Beauty would bring belonging. Beauty would offer security. Beauty would guarantee love. I lived in hyperawareness of blemishes, cellulite, split ends, and even my gait. I battled self-consciousness over the dark circles under my eyes and the alignment of my teeth. My prayer journals from that time featured sentence after agonizing sentence about weight, clothing, and even the pores on my nose. One morning, my roommate said, "You spend more time than anyone I know looking at your nose in the mirror."

Oh, my nose.

The wound is deep. Picture this: In ninth grade, the Most Gorgeous Boy in School sits right in front of me on the bus ride home. In slow motion, like something out of a romance movie, he turns around to me to say hello. And then he asks, "Why do you have all those little black dots on your nose? What *are* those?"

There was nowhere to run and hide.

What was I supposed to say? *Let me introduce you to my enormous pores?* They are pores. They are blackheads. They are the worst feature on my substantial nose!

"I don't know," I say, mortified.

His wide eyes and furrowed brow lean in closer. "Do I have them on *my* nose? Gross! Look at my nose, do I have them, too?" This actually happened. I could not make this up. I lean, in response, toward the Most Gorgeous Boy in School, noses nearly touching, not for any kind of first kiss, but to make sure his nose wasn't as hideous as mine.

"You're fine," I report. "Your nose is perfect."

I cried in my bedroom that night right into the lavender-scented pillowcase.

I hated my nose. I hated its size and the fact that it had pores large enough for people to see from afar. Could I get a new one? People surgically transformed their noses into tiny, pointy little things, and the magazines let me know about it in every grocery store checkout line.

I didn't get a new one. I kept this nose. But like I said, the wound is substantial. It may have been just a silly day on the sweat-smelly bus, but the insecurity it brought wasn't silly at all. The nose symbolized much more; it became a metaphor for everything I hated about my body. So when I recently read on Twitter *TIME's* claim that a study had determined the perfect nose ("slightly up-turned with an angle of 106 degrees"), I recalled the pain of my youth.[1] Well, first I felt sarcastic. (Thank goodness we found this out, people! Now we can really move forward as a culture!) Then I recalled the pain.

I recalled how I sent my own nose into hiding, and I wondered how many other girls read *TIME*'s report. I considered the implications of telling young women that there's a perfect "nasal tip rotation and projection" that is now and forevermore out of reach except by surgery. So far, apparently Kate Middleton, Scarlett Johansson, and Jessica Biel have achieved this perfection,[2] but we can all copy them if we have the financial means.[3] I'm seriously thinking that if the human skin were transparent, we'd all compare liver shape and pancreas rotation and claim a hierarchy of organ beauty. We would. We really would.

I tell my teenage daughter about the nose report from *TIME* in order to talk about how absurd it is, but she immediately grabs her nose and says, horrified, "Do *I* have a big nose?"

I throw my hands in the air and insist, "Nobody has a big nose. It's just a nose. It's for smelling things."

My younger daughter flares her little nostrils like an over-heated bull and says, "I love the smell of the cold, clean air."

Yes, my child! This is what the nose is for: smelling cold, clean air, gardenias, coffee and bacon, freshly mowed grass, and the salty ocean breeze. The nose is for snuggling into your loved ones and breathing in their scent. The nose isn't for measuring, comparing, or showcasing. It's for smelling—buttery yeast rolls, the new pages of a book, the dark, rich earth.

It's for storing precious memories of your childhood so that years later, you'll catch the scent of something and be brought right back here to that wonderful point in time. It might be the mustiness of the playing cards Grandma brought out or the way a cat's fur smells after she preens herself. It might be the aroma of your mother's pot roast or the smoky hot scent of the campfire.

That's what I hope my daughters think about when they consider their noses.

But me? My morning routine at that time included agonizing over my face. Squeezing, covering in thick foundation, and powdering comprised my daily routine in an attempt to send my nose into hiding. The rest of my face endured the assault of plucking, tweezing, rubbing, and steaming. And this was just for my *face*. The rest of my body invited a whole different set of insecurities.

As soon as my teen years approached, everything was about dieting to ensure a smaller waist, thighs, and hips. I stood in front of the mirror and wept at my growing hips and flabby arm fat. My appearance dominated my thoughts from the moment I gazed in the mirror in the morning till I prepared myself for bed with expensive lotions that promised to reduce the size of my pores and magically repair my skin in the night.

So I thought about myself all day long.

Not about Jesus, but *me*.

I thought about sitting the right way so I would look thinner. I thought about whether or not my foundation was working. I thought about whether I walked in an attractive way with good posture. I was so self-conscious that merely walking down the street meant I feared the gaze of anyone in my path.

Even as an adult, I retained some of these same patterns. As I read Ephesians 2:6 and considered my position as seated with Christ, I wondered how that verb, seated, might change how I felt about my appearance.

I was tired of all the insecurity. I was so tired of *myself*. I began to search the Scriptures, especially the Psalms, and I found that when David felt the most insecure, he fixed his eyes on something other than himself. He even claimed in Psalm 27:4, "One thing I ask from the Lord, this only do I seek: that I may dwell in the house of the Lord all the days of my life, to gaze on the beauty of the Lord and to seek him in his temple."

David *gazed* at the Lord's beauty. He fixed his eyes on Jesus. David took his eyes off himself.

Could it be true that I was beautiful because Christ is beautiful, and as I gazed at Him in my mind, could I stop fixating on my own face and body? In my imagination, I turned in my seat in the heavenly realms to Jesus just as I do in the morning when I turn my face

SEATED PEOPLE DON'T WORRY ABOUT THEIR APPEARANCE BECAUSE THEY ARE TOO BUSY ADORING THE BEAUTY OF THE KING.

up to the warm sun shining through the kitchen window. I thought about who God is and how He loves me.

I have no idea what Jesus looks like, but in my mind, it's all warmth and light and love at this table. I think of Jesus as having the most beautiful sparkling eyes. I think of a presence that wraps me up in His arms. I think of myself becoming illuminated within by this overwhelming, powerful, joyous, loving Christ. I'm caught up in the beauty of it.

I'm in my seat with such beauty around me. I adore Jesus and I'm not thinking about my nose. I can worship Jesus and stop idolizing artificial notions of beauty.

Within the last few years, I made the transition from agonizing over my appearance to *adoring* Jesus. Seated people don't worry about their appearance because they are too busy adoring the beauty of the King. They don't agonize; they adore.

As stated in Hebrews 12:2, we fix "our eyes on Jesus, the pioneer and perfecter of faith." Instead of thinking about our appearance, we fix our eyes on God. Is it that simple?

—⁂—

For my doctoral research at the University of Michigan, I studied the emotion of shame in literature, the most self-conscious and self-obsessed emotion humans can experience. I learned how, when we live in a state of this kind of self-consciousness, we believe that *everyone is looking at us and evaluating us*. More important, we live in a state of self-evaluation all day long.

Before the rise of social media, we only had the stares of the few people in our immediate surroundings to worry about. But today, Instagram, Facebook, Snapchat, and Twitter only compound our agony; we feel like we must be "camera ready" at all times because anyone can take our photo, tag us, and post it online. If you were even a bit nervous about your appearance before, now you're terrified about it. In other words, our current cultural moment invites shame at all times; we're gazing at others and ourselves through our phones and computers in a constant stream of photos.

How can we stop thinking about ourselves all the time? How can we stop fixating on our appearance and instead "fix our eyes" on Jesus? As I look back on my journey of healing from self-consciousness that culminated in a fuller understanding of being seated in Christ, I remembered two concepts that slowly delivered me from this obsession with my appearance.

The first seed of truth came to me one summer when I was working at Camp Greystone. I'll never forget the afternoon I was walking to the camp office from the dining hall. A visiting pastor's wife grabbed me by the arm and said, "I just wanted to tell you that you have a very loving face."

A very loving face.

I stood there and thought, "Loving? What about beautiful? I want a *beautiful* face." The sweet woman explained that when she saw me interacting with people, she could see God's love in me. In my face! This face that I didn't like! Some great shift occurred in my heart that moment, and even now, that compliment on that hot summer day, with sweat coming down my imperfect and blotchy face, is one of the favorites I've ever received.

I want a loving face that reflects the beauty of Christ.

That intention—to have a *loving* face instead of a beautiful one—changed me. My face was a mirror that no longer reflected *me*; people could look at me and see Jesus. I started to think about beauty differently that summer. That summer, I stopped checking the mirror so much, being insecure about my funny legs that turned at strange angles or wishing I looked like anyone else. I had a *loving face* that could express the heart of Jesus to others. That's what mattered. That's what I wanted.

When I'm seated with Christ, I am so secure that I can just love people through my appearance. I can look at people with God's love beaming through my face. I can use my eyes and my smile to love people. I can, dare I say, use my whole face, even my nose.

YOUR BEAUTY ENTHRALLS JESUS. TAKE A MOMENT AND ENJOY THAT SENTENCE. YOUR BEAUTY ENTHRALLS JESUS.

—◊◊◊—

The next seed of truth God taught me is found in an often-overlooked Bible verse. It's from Psalm 34:5 and simply says, "Those who look to him are radiant; their faces are never covered with shame." On three different occasions, I whispered a prayer to Jesus, "Help me be radiant today because I just feel so ugly." On each of those three days, a different person approached me and said, "Heather, I don't know what it is about you, but you look absolutely *radiant*!" It was as if God heard that prayer and used the very words I prayed to Him in the mouths of others so I would know He was listening and cared for me.

Psalm 34:5 had become so important to me that on our wedding day, I had a soloist sing the Twila Paris song "How Beautiful," because of a line she uses about a radiant bride. I was the *radiant* bride who once hated her appearance.

These moments between Jesus and me span across my adult life and show me His loving pursuit of me as His radiant bride. I recently read Psalm 45:11 where we're told, "let the king be enthralled by your beauty." Enthralled, by the way, means an "overwhelming longing for and fascination with."

Your beauty enthralls Jesus. Take a moment and enjoy that sentence.

Your beauty enthralls Jesus.

Over the years, I continued to pray that I would be "radiant" because I loved Jesus. The concepts of having a *loving face* and a *radiant face* made me embrace my facial characteristics and, in fact, my whole body. I'm enthralling. I'm fascinating. This is so much better than being culturally beautiful. This earthly vessel, after all, was made to love and serve. I could rest in the truth that I was radiant; I believe it by faith and accept it as true, no matter how much weight I have to lose or how many blemishes I'm treating.

I'm seated with Christ, gazing at a King who is enthralled by my beauty. This King loves my face and body, and He sends others into my life who love these things just as He does. For example, on one of the first dates with the gorgeous young man who became my husband, he casually asked, "Do you know what I love most of all out of all your features?"

"What? My eyes? My mouth?" I said, batting my eyelashes and puckering my lips.

"Your nose! It's so adorable. I just love your *nose*."

This happened. This happened on a date.

Nobody prompted him. Nobody shared the wound of the ninth grade bus ride. My nose—the thing that I hated the most—was the thing he loved the most. I think you might want to add this to your list of Ways You Know You Found Your Marriage Partner. This very nose, the one I hated and wanted to change, attracted my husband to me. It was as if God knew and cared about my insecurities, and He used that pastor's wife and my future husband to let me know that my face was actually something special.

It's true: I'm enthralling. I'm fascinating.

And you are, too.

God continues to heal me from obsessing over myself. I ask God for the privilege of reflecting His love *through my appearance*. Perhaps this face will draw someone who needs to know Him. Perhaps this smile will bring a hurting soul some comfort. Perhaps my eyes will draw my students in and let them experience the love of God. When I walk up on a stage to speak or when I enter the classroom to teach, I'm no longer self-conscious as I whisper to Jesus, "Help me radiate Your love through my appearance."

Recently, a neighbor said she loved that I wasn't trim and all made up every day because it allowed her to connect with me as a normal, average person. My appearance fostered an approachability and comfort that has served me well in ministry and teaching. As I thought about her comments, I made a list of the people who love and inspire me most of all—the ones I feel comfortable around and who help me to be myself. I realized they aren't attractive by the culture's standards. I also considered how some of the most spiritually influential and powerful people in the world—those remembered most for their love and service to Jesus—do not have anything about them to attract us physically by magazine standards. They are often wrinkled and old, like Mother Teresa, or bald and stout, like C. S. Lewis. If you think about the warm, soft, doughy arms of a loving mother or grandmother, you might stop wishing for sculpted triceps as I did.

WHEN I THINK ABOUT THIS MAGNIFICENT, SUBLIME BEAUTY OF WHAT WAS INSIDE OF JESUS' EARTHLY BODY, I'M SO CONSUMED WITH HIS QUALITIES THAT I STOP THINKING ABOUT MY OLD STANDARDS OF BEAUTY.

To add a bit of research into the mix, you might want to read a study published in the academic journal *Perception*. In 2004, a team from the department of psychology in Dublin's Trinity College published their research results about beauty. They discovered that what attracts us isn't beauty as much as *familiarity*; in other words, the more we see a face, the more beautiful and attractive it becomes—regardless of its features.[4] This explains why strangers who might seem unattractive become more beautiful to us over time; the more we see a face, the more we find it engaging.

I loved hearing about this research because I realized that typical standards of beauty have little (or nothing) to do with whether or not people find us attractive. Maybe this will change how you're thinking about those things you wish were different about your body; the more we see you—even those parts you don't love about yourself—the more we find ourselves attracted to you.

Are you beginning to realize that what your culture deems as beautiful isn't the correct understanding of beauty at all? Are you wondering if, up to this point in your life, you've focused on something so inconsequential and arbitrary? I'm beginning to realize that I've misunderstood beauty all my life, especially when I remember that Jesus Himself was not attractive. We're told in Isaiah 53:2–3 of our coming Messiah, Jesus Christ:

> He had no beauty or majesty to attract us to him,
> nothing in his appearance that we should desire him.
> He was despised and rejected by mankind,
> a man of suffering, and familiar with pain.
> Like one from whom people hide their faces
> he was despised, and we held him in low esteem.

When I read this passage, I feel very tenderly toward Jesus. I feel like He understands. The passage says that Jesus had "nothing in his appearance to attract us to him," and in fact, He was someone "from whom people hide their faces." This is a man who wasn't beautiful to the watching world.

But think about this: Jesus is the "radiance of God's glory and the exact representation of his being" (Hebrews 1:3). Within Jesus, a beauty more majestic and more notable than any other person in the entire history and future of mankind rests.

When I think about this magnificent, sublime beauty of what

was inside of Jesus' earthly body, I'm so consumed with His qualities that I stop thinking about my old standards of beauty. Think of it this way: When you stand before the great ocean, gaze down into the depths of the Grand Canyon, or lie in the cool grass underneath a night sky of shooting stars, you don't think about yourself. These sublime states of wonder deliver you from self-consciousness and self-focus.

Sublime experiences—that coupling of fear and wonder because the thing before you is just so awesome—take you out of the center of your world. There's something better, deeper, truer, and more powerful than you. If you remember your image of yourself as a Knight of the Round Table—battle ready for a great adventure—you can begin to experience the sublime kingdom living that takes you outside of yourself.

You can't think about your mascara when your mind is filled with God's grandeur. Try it. You just can't.

Something even more astonishing, however, is that this same mysterious beauty resides in us because we are clothed with Christ's righteousness (Isaiah 61:10), filled with the Holy Spirit (Ephesians 5:18), and hidden in Christ (Colossians 3:3). The beauty of Jesus resides within us this very moment. That beauty that surpasses any earthly beauty belongs to Jesus Christ with whom all the fullness of the Deity lives in bodily form (Colossians 2:9). With Christ in us, we are beautiful. We are beautiful indeed because Jesus emanates from within us. Christ's fragrance metaphorically exudes from our bodies. In 2 Corinthians 2:15, we know we are the "aroma of Christ." Remember that we are seated with Christ and in Christ. When people look at us, we can imagine that we are completely covered by Christ's righteousness. With this covering, I think about Him instead of me. I'm *in* Him, and "I no longer live" (Galatians 2:20). Everything becomes about Jesus living His resurrected life through my face and body.

As I continue to meditate on these truths, I remember that when I'm seated with Christ, I'm then sent out for good works, including those appointed for me as described in 2 Corinthians 5:20. I'm "Christ's ambassadors, as though God were making an appeal through [me]." I keep my eyes on Jesus, and then I go out into the world as a radiating presence of Christ. My face represents His love. My body puts His love into action.

And finally I remember 1 Samuel 16:7: "The Lord does not look at things people look at. People look at the outward appearance, but the Lord looks at the heart." I look at others and myself with new eyes. When I'm seated with Christ, I can see others with His kind of perception, not my own.

The spell has been broken. I finally see the truth about my face and yours.

—⁂—

When I look in the mirror, I feel *radiant*. I feel *loving*. I still wear makeup because it's fun and artful. I still treat blemishes and use products that help my skin, but it's not because I feel ugly. It's because I feel beautiful, and I want to care for my skin.

This year, I lost a lot of weight because I began to walk with my neighbor and intentionally ate healthier. I found that I began to enjoy moving my body and eating nutritious foods. It gave me more energy and an elevated mood, and so I kept walking and eating to support my health with more fruits and vegetables and less cake and potato chips.

I found that having lost weight, I could do more things with my body. My knees no longer hurt; I slept better; I could fit into my pants; and I had triple the energy. That made me so happy because my body and health wouldn't become a limitation. When motivated by this focus, instead of hating my body and seeking cultural beauty, I find it feels fun and joyful instead to seek health. God began to use my special seat at His table to purify my motivation in seeking health, to help me accept my body type and face, and to release me from thinking about it so much.

As I write that sentence, I'm amazed that after a lifetime of struggle with overeating and weight gain, I did not find the power and motivation to improve my health until I truly believed I was seated in the heavenly realms. The energy, security, and acceptance that the Holy Spirit brought into my heart through Ephesians 2:6 changed everything about me including eating habits (I didn't need food to solve my loneliness or fear), my exercise (I didn't need a thin body to earn a seat with the beautiful people; I was already seated at the table, so I could just enjoy physical activity), and my attitude about clothing and makeup (it's now an art form and not an attempt to gain a seat at the table).

However, take caution. When I began to lose weight and receive compliments for my appearance, I was tempted to base my identity on this. I think about the number of photos of young girls with pouty lips and luscious hair that parade through the social media feed. It's a constant stream of self-focused photographs to present a false kind of beauty to the world. It

BUT WHEN WE'RE SEATED IN CHRIST, WE GAZE AT JESUS AND EMBRACE OUR UNIQUE AND BEAUTIFUL APPEARANCE BY KEEPING THE KING AT THE CENTER OF OUR GAZE, NOT OUR OWN APPEARANCE.

seems we can't win: Either we're obsessing over how bad we look, or we're exalting ourselves because of our cultural beauty. But when we're seated in Christ, we gaze at Jesus and embrace our unique and beautiful appearance by keeping the King at the center of our gaze, not our own appearance.

We know we've been "knit together" (Psalm 139) by Him for a special purpose, and this includes our appearance, right down to the pores on our nose. When I'm seated with Christ, I rejoice in my God-given appearance, but I don't exalt myself and idolize it; I walk about with a new freedom and joy because I'm "fearfully and wonderfully made." I take everything about my appearance— what I perceive as good or bad—and I turn it all into moments of worship.

I see myself differently.

I see you differently.

I look at you, and I see an exquisite creation. I see a radiant person, and I'm enthralled. I'm fascinated. I hope you feel it as I look at you. I hope you feel the love of Jesus through my face. As I go about the day, I remember that, with each person I spend time with, I'm in the presence of the most profoundly and radiantly beautiful creature who is made in God's image.

Because I'm seated with Christ, I don't need to agonize; I adore. I turn my face to Jesus and imagine that, at this table, we're so beautiful that there's not even a category for it. It's beyond beauty. It's beyond appearance.

As you sit as this table, you know how Jesus feels about you.

Set the scene in your mind: The Most Gorgeous One in the Universe announces He's enthralled by someone in the room. He wants to invite this one to sit down beside Him at the royal table. Where is she? Who is this person?

I imagine Jesus turns to the Father and points to you.

He says, "That's her. Isn't she radiant?"

You, radiant you, takes a seat in the heavenly realms with the King.

SIT AND SAVOR

—ᜄ—

Read Psalms 45 and 139.

1. What are you most insecure about regarding how you look? What bred this insecurity in you? What is your daily life like because of this insecurity?

2. List all the things you love about your appearance. If you're doing this with a group, it might feel awkward, but you can begin by saying, "I'd like to thank God for making me with_____" (write down a particular feature).

3. Describe the personality of a person who is not attractive by the world's standards. What makes this person beautiful to you?

4. How does it make you feel to know that the King is "enthralled by your beauty"? Have you ever felt truly beautiful? When? Who made you feel that way?

5. What do you think being beautiful will provide for you? What is it that drives your insecurities about weight, looks, or anything else about your body? If you "fixed" that thing, what do you think would happen?

CHAPTER 6

—⟳—

FROM AFFLUENCE TO ACCESS

*Command those who are rich in this present world not to
be arrogant nor to put their hope in wealth, which is so
uncertain, but to put their hope in God, who richly
provides us with everything for our enjoyment.*

—1 TIMOTHY 6:17

Money. I wanted money. I loved money.

All my life I pictured the "good life" as one that had a large, professionally decorated home, nice cars, exotic vacations, luxurious spa treatments, fine dining, and various status symbols of wealth: designer fashion, multiple vacation homes, and the comfort of having housekeepers and personal chefs.

Where did I get these ideas of this "good life"? It wasn't just from the movies and magazines. I had a taste of wealth by sitting at those tables that let me peer in on the rich and famous. Besides having the privilege of meeting the first President Bush for example, I've encountered oil tycoons and business leaders worth more than 10 billion dollars. Yes, I wrote *billion*.

I grew up in an affluent home and pictured the good life as one filled with the amenities I was used to. I grew up believing I was special because I perceived we were wealthy.

In my young mind, it was very glamorous. It wasn't unusual for me to go on shopping sprees with my generous and exuberant mother who could spend all the money she desired. We would walk into specialty boutiques and receive exclusive attention. I knew what brands were status symbols of wealth; I knew what it meant to have a fine, cultured taste. After a day of shopping, my mother and I would dine at wonderful restaurants in Old Town, Alexandria, where the owners doted on us.

This was the lavish lifestyle I dreamed of for my adult life and for my future children.

And it was within my reach.

I married an intelligent and talented man who was a sought-after organic chemist. Ashley took a lucrative job at the world's top pharmaceutical company as a research chemist. I was finishing a PhD, ready for the job market where I would become a prestigious and well-paid tenure track professor. We had all the money we wanted; our newlywed days were spent purchasing furniture for our adorable apartment in Ann Arbor, dining at the best restaurants, attending films and concerts, and buying new clothes and jewelry. I was on my way to having a seat at the wealthy table. I thought about purchasing fine art, luxury cars, and my dream home.

That was the seat that would offer happiness and security. That was the seat that would sustain me all the days of my life.

—⁓—

Within that first year of marriage, Ashley and I felt led by the Lord into full-time ministry to graduate students and professors. At the same time, we discovered I was pregnant with our first daughter (five years earlier than our plan). Instead of going on the job market that year—with all that money and all that prestige—I would stay home with a baby. We would now depend on the financial support of churches and ministry partners as we moved into nonprofit Christian ministry. I now had a campus pastor for a husband instead of a chemist; I now had a baby and a humble ministry instead of my long-planned university career. I would wait another seven years until I found myself in a college classroom again—after another baby and years of clinical depression.

I thought I could do it. I thought I was strong enough to leave my life of wealth and comfort, but I wasn't. Within my first year as a new mother, I experienced a depression so profound and so despairing that an entire team of medical doctors and a skilled counselor came to my aid. I sat there in the counselor's office during my first appointment, and I felt ugly, poor, and useless. I felt hopeless and suicidal.

It was on that day that my counselor, Dr. Hocott, kindly suggested that the accumulation of wealth is a false self or what I learned later is a "false resting place"[1] that breeds a soul-corroding idolatry. Dr. Hocott knew that I had left a life of wealth to embrace a new ministry calling, and he was the first person who gave me hope that a new identity in Christ was mine for the taking.

But who was I if I wasn't rich? Who was I if I couldn't sit with the wealthy and the powerful? Who was I if I couldn't accumulate more and more status symbols of affluence? I was shackled in the prison of affluence; my identity—so entangled in this web of wanting money—broke apart and left me in despair. Our marriage suffered as I blamed my husband—and then ultimately God—for ruining my life.

The journey of healing began in an airport as I cried about my new ministry calling. I whispered, "Please God, no. Please, God. I

GOD ORDAINS WHAT KIND OF WEALTH I WILL HAVE. COULD I ENTRUST THIS PART OF MY LIFE TO JESUS? COULD I AGREE THAT HE WAS IN CHARGE OF EVEN THIS?

can't do this. I'm going to be poor. I'm going to suffer. Please, God, help me." In that airport as I traveled for another ministry training session, I was torn apart inside. I knew that God was leading us to do this work, but the part of me that wanted to control and direct my own life raged against this new lifestyle. I sat waiting for my flight and flipped through my Bible. *Please Jesus, teach me. How am I going to do this?*

I read something astonishing in Deuteronomy, a book of the Bible I typically ignore. Tucked into this chapter of warning about forgetting the Lord, the text reads:

> You may say to yourself, "My power and the strength of my hands have produced this wealth for me." But remember the Lord your God, for it is he who gives you the ability to produce wealth, and so confirms his covenant, which he swore to your ancestors, as it is today. (Deuteronomy 8:17–18)

These were strange and simple verses that God used to break apart my understanding of wealth. Those are words I *did* say to myself. *I* would produce wealth for myself. What was so wrong with that?

I wanted to work hard, earn money, and build a comfortable life for myself, but here, I read the truth that it is God who gives the ability to produce wealth. It comes from Him, and it all belongs to Him. God, in fact, ordains what kind of wealth I will have. Could

I entrust this part of my life to Jesus? Could I agree that He was in charge of even this?

I read in Psalm 50:10 how everything in creation belongs to God, and He owns "the cattle on a thousand hills." It was in this airport, with a tear-stained face and anger in my heart about all I was giving up—the vacations, the wardrobe, fine dining, dream homes, luxury cars—that God also led me to 1 Timothy 6:17: "Command those who are rich in this present world not to be arrogant nor to put their hope in wealth, which is so uncertain, but to put their hope in God, who richly provides us with everything for our enjoyment."

I closed my eyes and prayed, *Please build my faith to believe this, Jesus. Please, Jesus. Help me believe that You can richly provide for me.* As I sat there in the airport, the Holy Spirit gently uncovered in my mind that I believed the lie that wealth would bring me peace, joy, and fulfillment. It would bring happiness and security. But here, I read and listened carefully to the command not to put my hope or identity in wealth, but to hope only in God because He "richly provides all things for my enjoyment."

How would my attitude toward money change if I really believed God controls wealth and the ability to produce it? Does He own everything? Does He really provide all things? All things for my enjoyment? Not for my basic needs, but for my *enjoyment*?

For years I had been learning how to trust God to provide everything I needed. And finally, one July day, I read that I was seated with Christ at the royal table with access to every spiritual blessing. Here, I had everything I needed. Why did it take me so long to stop fighting for a seat with the wealthy? Why did I believe that financial prosperity was the secret to a happy life?

I confessed to the Lord that my whole life was about fighting for a seat at the table of wealth and prosperity. Even after He had provided a lifetime of shelter, food, and clothing for me, I still wanted more and more prosperity. It was selfish. It was misguided. It was a lie I continued to believe. But that day with Ephesians 2:6, I thought about all the wealthy women in my life of whom I was so jealous—for their clothes, vacations, and beautiful homes. Now I thought of them as seated in Christ and appointed for those particular gifts.

I didn't feel jealous. I didn't compare myself to them because I knew I too was seated at the royal table. I knew that God had special gifts for me, too. I didn't need to compare myself to anyone because at this table, a knight has everything she needs to accomplish the King's mission for her life. God appoints and ordains the financial provision for my life. I can let go of this obsession; I can sit at the table and crush the idol of affluence.

I realized: *Seated people don't worry about affluence anymore because they know they have access to the riches of God.* I have *access* to the riches of God. They are available to me at all times. I memorized Philippians 4:19 where Paul writes, "My God will meet all your needs according to the riches of his glory in Christ Jesus."

All my needs.

I began a practice of writing down "all my needs." I have twenty years' worth of prayer journals that showcase God's provision of housing, clothing, transportation, and food. I even have recorded nonessential items that God provides for my enjoyment. I smile and burst out laughing when I think of how that same young woman who cried in the airport has since then traveled all over the nation on ministry assignments, dined in fabulous places, and worn many beautiful clothes given as gifts. That young woman has had more materially abundant living than you can imagine *because* of her ministry work. This calling has positioned her at the finest tables in the world.

But she finally didn't need those seats anymore.

—⁓—

The end of that sentence in Philippians 4:19 uses the phrase, "according to the riches of his glory in Christ Jesus." I coupled this phrase with the one in Ephesians 1:3 that says God has "blessed us in the heavenly realms with every spiritual blessing in Christ." As I thought deeply about riches and spiritual blessings, I lifted my eyes from material provisions to consider *spiritual riches.* I thought of eternal, unseen things that were more valuable than the richest objects or experiences on earth.

I thought about the fruit of the spirit in Galatians 5 and the riches of love, joy, and peace. I thought about the riches of Christ's righteousness applied to me. I thought of intimacy with God. I thought about the invitation to the table and the mission of those seated in the heavenly realms.

DID YOU NOTICE THAT IN ADDITION TO FORGIVENESS OF SIN, HEALING, REDEMPTION, AND THE EXPERIENCE OF LOVE AND COMPASSION, GOD SATISFIES OUR DESIRES WITH GOOD THINGS?

Oh, I was rich! I was rich beyond measure! I was overwhelmed that not only would Jesus provide these spiritual blessings, but He would also provide good things for my enjoyment in tangible forms. For example, in Psalm 103, we know the benefits of God, those intangible riches expressed in the first five verses. We read:

Praise the Lord, my soul;
    all my inmost being, praise his holy name.
Praise the Lord, my soul,
    and forget not all his benefits—
who forgives all your sins
    and heals all your diseases,
who redeems your life from the pit
    and crowns you with love and compassion,
who satisfies your desires with good things
    so that your youth is renewed like the eagle's.

Did you notice that in addition to forgiveness of sin, healing, redemption, and the experience of love and compassion, God "satisfies [our] desires with good things" to renew us? I love that our desires are *satisfied*—not just whetted. Next to that psalm in my worn, green Bible, I listed out all the ways I was rich with good things that God has provided just for me.

I even wrote about the blessings of birds. I'm rich in *birds*.

A dear neighbor and mentor, Sandy, and I were talking about our fascination with birds. In the woods behind our home, I can find snowy owls, barn owls, woodpeckers, and even eagles. By the kitchen window, the northern cardinals dance about all day. As Sandy and I shared a moment of wonder over birds, I remarked that God didn't have to make birds.

"And He didn't have to make them *sing*, either," she says. They seem placed here for such delight I can hardly bear it. Then my wise neighbor reminds me of the *riches* of it all. "You never have to worry about being rich," she says. "You have the riches of nature always available to you."

I think about the riches of nature. I think about my wonderful neighbor and the riches of wisdom. I think about the backyard feeder and the riches of cardinals robed in deep red. I think of the riches of family, laughter, vivid verbs, and wonderful friends. At this very moment, I'm rich in snowflakes, dark coffee, and fuzzy slippers. I'm rich in icy ponds and crackling icicles that make the houses seem swallowed in great jaws.

I'm rich in poetry books, old dusty journals, Bibles, new novels buried inside me, and Penn State students who write so honestly I sometimes cry when I grade their papers. I'm rich in professors who meet with me even though we only have forty-five minutes once a week to eat lunch together. I'm rich in neighborhood moms and dads who are raising children alongside my husband and me. I'm rich in Italian mamas who have adopted me as one of their own in my neighborhood.

God has poured out *all these riches* all over me as if knowing Him weren't enough. Jesus continues to redefine for me the definition of "riches" or "treasures." For example, In Proverbs 24:3–4, we read this: "By wisdom a house is built, and through understanding it is established; through knowledge its rooms are filled with rare and beautiful treasures." I wanted rare and beautiful treasures. Who wouldn't love a house like this?

PEOPLE FILLED EVERY ROOM, AND THEY WERE MORE PRECIOUS THAN ALL THE GOLD IN THE WORLD.

We hosted a big Christmas party for students recently. So many of them came to find me in the kitchen. They said, "Thank you for opening your home to us!" I remember how, years ago, I worried about the old carpets, outdated and damaged furniture, and mismatched plates. I wanted a stunning home, filled with all kinds of breathtaking things. I wanted those rare and beautiful treasures I see in magazines and in store windows. But that night, with all the people filling our living room and caroling, I remember that the "rare and beautiful treasures" are *people*. People filled every room, and they were more precious than all the gold in the world.

So I have every spiritual blessing in Christ, and now I can add the riches of *people* to my account. Even more, as I think about houses—and the fact that we still rent one here while other friends our age own property—I let this one statement in Psalm 90:1 settle deeply into my soul: "Lord, you have been our dwelling place." The Lord is my home. He is where I dwell. I'm with Christ and *in* Him at the royal table. *My home is inside of the Lord.* No matter where He moves me and whether I own homes or not, the Lord is my dwelling place.

My account increases: spiritual blessings, people, a home in God, and now what else?

Oh, there's more. There's so much more.

I was meditating on Psalm 84:11 where we read the audacious and nearly impossible-to-believe statement that "No good thing will he withhold from those whose walk is blameless."

This cannot be true. Are you thinking this? Are you mentally listing out all the things that the Lord has failed to provide for you? I am too. But guess what—I've learned this: If I pray for it, and God doesn't provide it, it means it wasn't a good thing or it wasn't a good thing for me right now. But even deeper than this simple platitude is the idea of "withholding." I read in John 3:34 that "God gives the Spirit without limit." Without limit! In other words, God does not withhold *Himself* from us. We can have all of Him that we want in an unlimited way.

Finally, when I think about how Jesus is my Good Thing, and how God promises in Psalm 84 to not withhold Him (the ultimate

Good Thing) from me, then suddenly I feel like the wealthiest woman in the world.

I have Jesus. I have all of Him. I have all I need and want at all times. My account just burst into the billions. I have Jesus. I'm indeed the richest one at the party.

—⁓—

My life looks nothing like I thought it would when I imagined my wealthy future. My seat in the heavenly realms didn't include some things I had once hoped for. I talk to Jesus about these things I sometimes dream about—travel, a certain house, a brand-new car. And then I read in 2 Corinthians 9:8 that "God is able to bless [me] abundantly, so that in all things at all times, having all that [I] need, [I] will abound in every good work." I underline all the "all" words.

All things. At all times. All that I need.

I have it *all*.

I'm seated in Christ, and I have everything.

And what about 1 Corinthians 3:21 where Paul writes that "all things are [ours]"? I finally believe it. I finally smile and nod in agreement when I read Psalm 31:19 where David writes, "How abundant are the good things that you have stored up for those who fear you, that you bestow in the sight of all, on those who take refuge in you." God will show His goodness to us; in fact, He has goodness stored up—in a great stockpile—for us.

People fighting for a seat at the table become consumed with wealth. They try to prove themselves with ever-increasing purchases and status symbols. They live in fear. They live in comparison. They cannot rejoice with the success or provision of others because they become jealous and angry about their own lives. They live in an impoverished mindset where they consider everything they lack instead of every way God has blessed them.

That was me, fighting for my seat at the rich person's table, but it became worse when we began to raise our daughters. I didn't believe that they were seated in Christ, too. I wanted them to have the finest things, and I was afraid of all they would miss out on without the shopping, the vacations, the glamorous living. When I read Ephesians 2:6, I placed my own daughters in their seats in the heavenly realms. God would provide for them. God would bless them. They would not miss out on anything.

I must continually remind myself of the truth of it. My friend Denise and I were walking together this morning. I had just read in Proverbs 28:20 that a "faithful person will be richly blessed, but one eager to get rich will not go unpunished." I confessed to the Lord that deep in my heart, I knew there were places in my heart that were, even after all this time and meditating on God's Word, "eager to get rich." I told Denise how I was writing a chapter in a book about my journey to feel seated in Christ at a royal table. We talked about all the status symbols of what it means to sit at the "Rich Table." We laughed as we walked about how ridiculous we sounded because of how arbitrary it all was, just like beauty. Last year, wealth meant a certain brand of yoga pants, a particular environmentally friendly car, or the right vacation spot. This year, it's the style of boots, purse, and headphones. Next year, it will be something else.

JESUS SAYS, "COME AND SEE."

When I think about arbitrary and shifting symbols of wealth and what I'm authorizing as the definition that I'm at the table, I gain a new perspective. Just as the spell of the beauty myth was broken, the enchantment about money dissolves when I examine the frenzy of people in different parts of the world to showcase whatever wealth means in that community. I can take my seat at Christ's table and, by faith, find contentment whether I'm managing many financial resources or struggling to pay for groceries. Just as Paul sat destitute in prison but knew a supernatural contentment and assurance of God's provision, I can trust God to care for my soul no matter what my financial situation.

What are my symbols now? A seated life sees riches as access to God's provision at all times. The measure of our wealth, then, is a measure of our dependence on Jesus. The wealthiest one is the most broken, the most humble, and the most God-reliant. I read Tolstoy's quote that "Wealth is the number of things one can do without" and I feel like I'm finally the new person my counselor said I could be.

Jesus has brought me so far.

Sometimes in my journal, when I feel the old ache rise up that I could be living a different, wealthier life, I recall the first recorded question that Jesus asks in the gospel of John. We see in John 1:38 that He turns around and asks the two disciples following Jesus, "What do you want?"

I love this question.

What do you want? What do you really want?

I love the disciples' answer even more. They essentially ask Jesus where He is staying. They want to be where Jesus is. They would leave *everything* to be in His presence.

So Jesus says, "Come and see."

When God asks, "What do you want?"—*What do you really want?*—I know the answer.

From deep within my heart I know that what I really want is to be with Jesus. Still, I write in my journal, *I want Jesus, but I'm scared. Is it really worth it to pursue God and not material things? Is Jesus enough?*

And God says: "Come and see."

As I'm seated with Christ, I begin to rejoice in Him, "as one rejoices in great riches" (Psalm 119:14). I can say that Jesus makes me "fully satisfied as with the richest of foods" (Psalm 63:5). It's been years of "coming and seeing" God's plan in this simple life.

—⁓—

It's thrilling to think of all the ways you might think about wealth differently now that you're seated in the heavenly realms. It's equally thrilling to recount all the ways God has provided for you. In Deuteronomy 2:7 we read, "the Lord your God has blessed you in all the work of your hands. He has watched over your journey through this vast wilderness. These forty years the Lord your God has been with you, and you have not lacked anything." When I look back on my life, it's absolutely true that I have not lacked anything.

The Lord your God has been with you, and you have not lacked anything.

As I'm seated at the table and gazing at my amazing God, I remember that one of His names is Jehovah-Jireh (Genesis 22:12–14): the God who provides. I need not worry about money again. I can stop fighting for a seat among the rich. And when God gives me special assignments that create material wealth as a by-product (writing, teaching, speaking), I surrender those new resources to Him. I ask God what to do with the money, and I learn to be Spirit-led. Wealth, I've learned, isn't wrong; my attitude toward it is what needed transformation. Now, I realize that I'm already at the greatest, most lavish table, and God will provide for all of my needs. He just asks me to "come and see."

I've come to my seat in the heavenly realms. As I sit in my seat, I know I have access to the riches of God's kingdom. He's a lavish

God. We're told in Ephesians 1:7–8 about the riches of God's grace that Christ "lavished on us." That Greek verb means to overwhelmingly supply to overflowing or to "abound in affluence." Because I have access to the riches of God's grace, I abound in affluence. Affluence, the very word that once imprisoned me, now means something so different. Now when I think about this lavish God who meets all of my needs, I know more fully the truth of Hebrews 4:16: I can "approach God's throne of grace with confidence, so that [I] may receive mercy and find grace to help [me] in [my] time of need." I tell Jesus everything about my "time of need," and He often and usually provides physically yes, but more beautiful still is the mercy and grace He gives me to experience His presence that is available to us at all times. I'm seated with Jesus, and He knows what I need.

SIT AND SAVOR

—⁓—

Read Philippians 4:19.

1. How have you seen that God has met "all your needs according to the riches of his glory in Christ Jesus"?

2. List ten ways you are rich that have nothing to do with money.

3. What do you think someone wealthier than you has that you do not have?

4. What attitudes about money did you grow up with? Tell the group what role money and the accumulation of wealth play in your daily life.

5. Do you see wealth as a resource to accomplish God's plans? If so, how does this help you think about money differently?

—⁜—

CHAPTER 7

FROM ACHIEVEMENT TO ABIDING

*Lord, you establish peace for us; all that we
have accomplished you have done for us.*

—ISAIAH 26:12

I magine being unknown and unproductive. Imagine embracing your own irrelevance and unimportance. Does this thought scare you? It terrifies me.

Achievement for me—and being recognized for it—was (and sometimes still is) one of the greatest strongholds in my life. Once I worked through the beauty and wealth issue with Jesus, I still did not know how to live like a seated person because of this lie: I believe that I am seated only when I am *achieving.* I believe I have a seat at the table if I receive recognition, honor, and importance because of what I accomplish.

If you look back on your own life, you might see that you, too, felt loved, important, and worthwhile if you were accomplishing something. In other words, what you offered the world was what made you special, not your intrinsic worth as a seated child of God. Like me, perhaps your life up to this point has been driven by goal-setting and achievement. You measure your worth by questions like these: "Am I a success? Am I important? Do I have a seat with these people in my career?"

What if your worth and importance were already decided and not based at all on what you were accomplishing? What if you were Mephibosheth—seated at the royal table, not for what you could offer but just because of a covenant promise? What if all this achievement isn't really what your heart wants after all?

Henry David Thoreau famously said, "We can spend our whole lives fishing only to discover in the end it wasn't fish we were after." I'll get to the point: our hearts don't really want *importance*; our hearts crave the righteousness of Christ that declares our *unconditional acceptance*.

It took a long time for me to learn this. I've been battling misplaced identity through achievement for most of my life. I know the exact moment the stronghold took root: I was seven years old at Washington Mill Elementary school in Alexandria, Virginia. My first grade class, along with the entire school, had been asked to write a simple essay about our love of trees for an Arbor Day contest. Over the loud speaker, the principal announced the winner of this essay contest.

Me! I won! From the whole school, they chose me.

I would travel to meet the governor and his wife and I would read my essay aloud to important people. I would wear a new dress with shiny black shoes. I would stand on a stage. Photographers would take my picture as I held a pine sapling in honor of Arbor Day.

That afternoon at recess, everyone wanted to play with *me*. Everyone wanted *my* attention. That feeling of belonging, of having a seat at the table, became a drug as powerful as anything in the world. From that day in first grade with Mrs. Mayo until just a few years ago, I did everything I could to win that spotlight through achievement. I wrote and spoke and earned the best grades. I traveled for oratory and debate, and I thought that as long as I kept achieving, I would find and keep what I've always dreamed of: a seat at the table. I kept pushing and pushing and pushing. Not only did I need to earn my seat at bigger and better tables, but I also had to keep my seat by continuing to prove I belonged.

—⁓—

At the University of Virginia, I worked hard for awards and recognition. At the University of Michigan, I worked even harder for awards and recognition. I thought: *I will earn that PhD and finally be at the smart person's table. I will earn teaching awards and attention for my writing. I will publish and speak and mentor. I will finally have a seat at the indispensable professors' table.*

Are you as tired as I am just reading those sentences? Oh, if only you knew. This kind of living nearly destroyed me as I clamored for a seat at the "professor table"; I would earn the PhD, secure a tenure-track job, earn tenure, publish prolifically, and then finally have my place at the table I've been waiting for all my life.

Early in this process, God reminded me that this economy of ranking, comparison, and superiority kept me imprisoned in a state of acute self-consciousness and self-absorption. Back then, I recognized how academia kept me toggling between feelings of superiority or inferiority (often within the same afternoon!) as I fought to

SEATED PEOPLE DON'T FOCUS ON ACHIEVEMENT ANYMORE. THEY ABIDE.

belong. I actually wrote my dissertation on shame and narcissism as a result. Now, ten years later, I still battle the tendency to self-evaluate and compare myself to others in my teaching. It doesn't stop there; I measure myself against other writers, other mothers, and other wives. Am I achieving enough by comparison?

When God reminds me that I already have a seat at the table, I begin to realize that seated people don't focus on achievement anymore. They abide.

They *abide.*

This abiding—instead of achieving—revolutionized my life.

When I read John 15:5 in the context of being seated in Christ, I stop thinking about identity in terms of achievement. Jesus says this: "I am the vine; you are the branches. If you remain in me and I in you, you will bear much fruit; apart from me you can do nothing." That Greek verb for "remain" means to "abide, to stay in place, to be continually present with." Jesus promises that as we stay continually present with Him, we will *bear much fruit.*

Much fruit: the fruit of good character and increasing Christlikeness (Galatians 5) and the fruit of good works and new believers. Jesus says, "Follow me and I will send you out to fish for people" (Matthew 4:19). When I'm abiding in Christ, my life will begin to accomplish incredible things. But it's not about achievement anymore that determines my identity.

Seated people abide. They remain seated. They enjoy Jesus and naturally and inevitably live Ephesians 2:10 where we know we're "created in Christ Jesus to do good works, which God prepared in advance for us to do." I'm free to complete these tasks from a position of security. I have already received the fullness of Christ, His righteousness, and His power to accomplish all He calls me to do. Christ won a place for me, and I am seated in Him and with Him. I can stop fighting to win a spot.

As I shared earlier, this realization changes how I approach all aspects of my life. Just like with seeking health and finding freedom from affluence, when I live as one already seated, my motivations in my work

IT FEELS SO FREE TO LIVE A SEATED LIFE.

and ministry are genuine. Christ's love is my purpose, not a need to belong somewhere, earn a title, or feel superior in some way. Now freed from self-absorption and continual self-evaluation about whether I'm enough, I have energy and confidence to love others well and serve the world with joy. I do not fight for a seat at the table; whether I fail or succeed against some arbitrary standard no longer matters.

I'm already there. It feels so free to live a seated life.

———

When I think about Ephesians 2:10 and how it says I'm created in Christ Jesus "to do good works, which God prepared in advance for [me] to do" and how the good work that Jesus began in me will be carried out to completion (Philippians 1:6), I finally relax into my seat in the heavenly realms. God has good works prepared for me that look nothing like the good works prepared for other people. If you look closely at Hebrews 12:1–2, it says that as we fix our eyes on Jesus, we run the race marked out for us. Not anyone else's—just my race. My accomplishments. My good works. My life.

Let me revise that: I'm crucified with Christ, so everything that happens to me are *His* accomplishments through me, *His* good works lived out through me, and *His* resurrected life lived through me. Even more important, these good works aren't mine individually. Together we bear fruit for God. We "strive together" as noted in Philippians 1:27; we aim, like Jesus prayed for us in John 17, to "be one" and to "be brought to complete unity" (vv. 21–23). To-gether, "we might bear fruit for God" (Romans 7:4). We "spur one another on" as we bear fruit for God (Hebrews 10:24).

This concept of together bearing fruit rips apart my radical indi-vidualism, my personal goals, and my independent, high-achieving heart. Instead, I see myself as part of a body; I'm collaborating, inter-dependent, and deeply involved with others. We bear fruit together. I might not ever receive the credit. I might remain hidden, anony-mous, and deprived of recognition. I might find my name dissolving into a group effort that never recognizes my contribution.

This kind of thinking—that I don't have to be the one recog-nized—seems like a terrible death of self. I've spent forty years try-ing to be remarkable, notable, and remembered. I keep a powerful quote with me at all times in my phone that I read sometimes when I feel the old tug of wanting importance or recognition through my accomplishments. It says this:

> Whatever would render us remarkable amongst the others, and for which credit would be gained among men, as if we were the only people who could do it, this should be shunned by us. For by these signs the deadly taint of vainglory will be shown to cling to us.[1]

Do you resist this quote because of the idea of not trying to be "remarkable" in comparison to others or not trying to gain credit? This thinking contradicts my entire upbringing. Isn't the point to stand out, to be the best, and to get all the glory for yourself that you can? I lie awake at night, thinking about this quote. I think about what it means to raise exceptional children. I think about how, all my life, I was taught to gain credit and to achieve. The early church fathers don't suggest we shun receiving credit and appearing remarkable; no, they declare we turn from these behaviors as soon as we believe "we were the only people who could do it."

It is God who gives us our talents. It is He who gives us our intelligence. I have nothing within me that wasn't given to me by God. With these truths, pride (vainglory), cannot take root. I also remember in Philippians 2:6–7 how Jesus who, "being in very nature God, did not consider equality with God something to be used to his own advantage; rather, he made himself nothing by taking the very nature of a servant."

Could I take on the very nature of a servant? Could I proclaim, as the prophet Isaiah did, "Your name and renown are the desire of [my] heart" (Isaiah 26:8)? Seated people can agree to turn from fame and importance. Seated people can, in the words of Henri Nouwen, embrace their irrelevance. He states:

> I am deeply convinced that the Christian leader of the future is called to be completely irrelevant and to stand in this world with nothing to offer but his or her own vulnerable self. That is why Jesus came to reveal God's love. The great message that we have to carry, as ministers of God's word and followers of Jesus, is that God loves us not because of what we do or accomplish, but because God has created and redeemed us in love and chosen us to proclaim that love as the true source of human life.[2]

We have been created and redeemed in love and chosen to proclaim that love. We offer our "irrelevant" and "vulnerable self" to others. We are seated. We abide instead of achieve, and we find a new way to think about our work and our goals. We accomplish many wonderful things, but it's not about certifying or creating an

SETTING THE LORD BEFORE ME HAS EVERYTHING TO DO WITH THINKING ABOUT JESUS, TALKING TO JESUS, LEARNING FROM JESUS THROUGH THE BIBLE, AND INVOLVING JESUS IN MY DAILY AFFAIRS. I STOP WORRYING ABOUT WHAT I'M ACCOMPLISHING, AND I FOCUS ON JESUS.

identity for ourselves. It's not about guaranteeing a seat at the table.

Seated people abide in Christ, and good works come like the inevitable fruit that comes from the vine. But how? Abiding in Christ means continually setting Jesus before me in my mind. In Psalm 16, David writes, "I keep my eyes always on the Lord. With him at my right hand, I will not be shaken."

Setting the Lord before me has everything to do with thinking about Jesus, talking to Jesus, learning from Jesus through the Bible, and involving Jesus in my daily affairs. It's a mindset and an attitude of praise, worship, thanksgiving, confession, supplication, and consultation as I ask Him for wisdom for every decision. I stop worrying about what I'm accomplishing, and I focus on Jesus.

I think about growing my soul. And then, fruit comes.

—⁂—

Sometimes, I walk around my home or campus and I repeat Galatians 2:20: "I have been crucified with Christ and I no longer live, but Christ lives in me. The life I now live in the body, I live by faith in the Son of God who loved me and gave himself for me." I say to Jesus: *I belong to You. I surrender my dreams and ambitions and goals. Work in me what is pleasing to You. Help me live by faith and abide in You. I'm covered by Your righteousness and have every-thing I need. I'm seated in Christ. Let this day bear fruit for You.*

I keep praying this because the old me keeps trying to achieve. But I know the truth: It's about abiding, not accomplishing. It's about being seated at the table and now being free to be myself.

My identity is secure in Christ. My new "goal" is to keep abiding in Christ and to enjoy the adventure of what comes next in ministry, writing, and teaching. While I have many months and even years that allow me to live in temporary victory over the need to achieve, the stronghold returns whenever I enter a new job, a new ministry assignment, or a new publishing opportunity. I still con-

MAYBE GOD KNOWS THAT I NEED SEASONS OF TOTAL EMPTINESS, NO FRUIT, NOT EVEN BLOSSOMS, IN ORDER TO GET MY ROOTS DEEP AND STRONG.

fess that I want to feel important and recognized. I place the truth continually in front of my conscious mind. I must daily remember that I'm seated and abiding. I can stop fighting so hard.

I found a wonderful example in nature to help explain abiding. A few years ago, Ashley transformed the right side of our backyard into a berry farm for my Mother's Day present. He prepared the soil and planted blueberries, strawberries, raspberries, and black-berries. I imagined all the pies, smoothies, jams, and cobblers I would make. I pictured all the fresh berries I'd freeze for the winter. That first summer, I bragged to my neighbors—gardening experts and part of this Centre County farming community—all about my berries. I waved my arm in a swooping gesture as if to say, "Behold, my fruit!" as I pointed out the blossoms emerging on my fruit plants.

"Oh no!" the neighbors cried. "You cannot let that fruit produce! You must take off every single bloom. You need to remove that fruit! Pinch off the blossoms, too. Do *not* let those plants produce! Not this summer, and not next summer either."

All week, we'd been so happy about those blueberries and those ripening strawberries. There was *no way* I was going to destroy that young fruit and those beautiful blossoms. Who were these people to suggest I would have to be patient for two more summers? (I realize that most of my friends know this about berry plants. I somehow missed the information.)

"You have to. You just *have* to do it. Make your husband do it," my understanding friend said. "But it has to happen."

This counterintuitive and destructive move would make my plants thrive. If I take away the fruit, the plant directs the energy and nutrients to the most important part of the plant: the root system. A new berry plant needs a few years to make an indestructible foundation of roots. *Then*, we can enjoy the fruit. It would take three summers.

So that next morning, Ashley prepared our plants for abundance by deliberately diminishing them. All night I'd been thinking of what my friend said as I sat there with my mouth hanging open, refusing to believe the truth about my plants. My gardening friend said with such love and wisdom: "You've lived here three years, right? Weren't the first two hard? And now, in your third year, everything's going so well."

I thought about the principle of *three years*. Maybe it was true. Maybe God knows that we need seasons of total emptiness, no fruit, not even blossoms, in order to get our roots deep and strong. I thought about marriage, of raising those babies to toddlers, of moving to new places and starting new jobs. I thought about years waiting for manuscripts to be published, friendships to form, and communities to thrive. It never all came together that first year, and maybe not even the second. But the third year? Fruit *did* come.

My berry plants remind me to look at my life and realize that in those years when nothing seems to happen, where nothing seems to bloom in my life, I'm putting down indestructible roots.

Seated people focus on the roots, not the fruits.

As I stayed in my seat in the heavenly realms, I imagined Jesus doling out the "good works" set apart for me to do. I recalled in Philippians 2:13 how "it is God who works in you to will and to act in order to fulfill his good purpose." He's working in me to give me the desire and the ability to bear the fruit He's ordained for my life. I remembered how Jesus says, in John 15:16, "You did not choose me, but I chose you and appointed you so that you might go and bear fruit—fruit that will last—and so that whatever you ask in my name the Father will give you." In other words, God chose me and appointed me to bear fruit. He designs this fruit. I do not.

SEATED PEOPLE SIMPLY ENJOY WORK AS A PLEASING SACRIFICE, AN ACT OF WORSHIP, AND AS A WAY TO ENJOY GOD.

Do you realize what this means? Do you understand the far-reaching, all-consuming implications of this for someone like me who's been in bondage to achievement all her life? It means that I'm free. Nothing's at stake for me in my identity anymore. I'm seated in Christ—the highest achievement I'll ever have (and I didn't even do it—Jesus did)—so everything I do is now an overflow of my intimacy with Jesus at the table. I stop the frenzied clamoring to achieve because Jesus has already chosen and designed the particular good works for my life.

So what will I do, and how will I live? Seated people, I'm learning, simply enjoy work as a pleasing sacrifice, an act of worship, and as a way to enjoy God. They see work as a way to bless other people and advance the kingdom of God. Work becomes about aiding human flourishing all over the world. It becomes about proclaiming the gospel in the context of whatever work is happening.

Seated people steward well their talents and gifting; they maximize the resources God gives them and then, by the power of the Holy Spirit, produce much fruit. We become like those described in 1 Thessalonians 1:3. Paul writes here, "We remember before our God and Father your work produced by faith, your labor prompted by love, and your endurance inspired by hope in our Lord Jesus Christ." Work comes from *faith*, prompted by *love*. It does not originate from a desire to achieve, to make a name for myself, or to feel important.

But what is this work? What is this labor? I know at least one thing for sure about this fruit and these "good works" set apart for me; these works are all about introducing people to Jesus. When I read 2 Corinthians 5:17–21, I get so excited. Paul writes:

Therefore, if anyone is in Christ, the new creation has come: The old has gone, the new is here! All this is from God, who reconciled us to himself through Christ and gave us the ministry of reconciliation: that God was reconciling the world to himself in Christ, not counting people's sins against them. And he has committed to us the message of reconciliation. We are therefore Christ's ambassadors, as though God were making his appeal through us. We implore you on Christ's behalf:

Be reconciled to God. God made him who had no sin to be sin for us, so that in him we might become the righteousness of God.

I have a ministry; God gave it to me. It's called the "ministry of reconciliation" meaning that everywhere I go—neighborhood, workplace, natural pathways—God is using me to make an appeal to other people. I'm an *ambassador*.

This sounds so prestigious, so very high-achieving, doesn't it? Think about how dignified and difficult such a career actually is. To become your country's ambassador to a foreign country, for example, you must prove exceptional skill, pass many exams and security clearances, showcase a record of exemplary service to your nation, and demonstrate expert knowledge of the language and culture of another country.

Me? I took my seat in the heavenly realms and received my title from Jesus. I'm an ambassador to the greatest King in the universe.

—ɷ—

Essentially, being seated in Christ means I stop achieving and start abiding. When I abide—and bear the fruit that God appoints for me—whether larger or small things, hidden or displayed things—I no longer compare myself to others or worry about the great accomplishments of others. I'm free from jealousy and comparison when I'm seated in Christ.

Recently, a friend of mine asked me how I was handling the success of another woman's fame over her shame and intimacy research (my same research interests from my days at the University of Michigan). This woman was going viral on YouTube, selling millions of books, and appearing on Oprah's *Super Soul Sunday*. My friend said,

SEATED PEOPLE LOVE THE SUCCESS OF OTHERS; THEY REJOICE THAT THIS BEAUTIFUL THING HAPPENED, AND IT DIDN'T HAVE TO BE THROUGH THEM.

"That could have been you! Aren't you so mad? You studied the same thing. You know the same things as she does."

I nodded and smiled a real, honest smile. "I am so happy that work is out there." That's what I felt in my heart.

Can you believe this supernatural change in me? In *The Freedom of Self-Forgetfulness,* Tim Keller talks about coming to the point where you stop thinking about yourself and comparing your successes or failures to others. You do things out of love because you're so secure and accepted in Christ. You aren't trying to prove you're special. Keller writes:

> Wouldn't you like to be the skater who wins the silver, and yet is thrilled about those three triple jumps that the gold medal winner did? To love it the way you love a sunrise? Just to love the fact that it was done? For it not to matter whether it was their success or your success. Not to care if they did it or you did it. You are as happy that they did it as if you had done it yourself—because you are just so happy to see it.[3]

Keller further explains that when folks live in the freedom of the gospel, they no longer attach accomplishment or failure to their *identity.* They experience joy when others succeed because they're just so happy to see it accomplished. Being seated with Christ, I finally feel this way as I walk around the English department and my neighborhood. I rejoice when others succeed.

Only Jesus could do this in me and transform me like this.

As if God wanted me to really understand this freedom from achievement, I learned even more about this from something the lead singer of the band Tenth Avenue North said at a concert. I had been researching the dangers of narcissism in leaders. Christian leadership, in many ways, can breed a kind of excessive self-focus and self-promotion.

When Mike Donehey, the band's lead singer speaks, he seems so humble and unconcerned with how he's coming off. In fact, he tells the crowd he's changed. Donehey claims that in the early days of the band's success, he'd pray before concerts, "God, please use us. Please use us!"

"I don't pray that anymore," he says. "Now, I ask God to *just move*, and it doesn't have to be through us. It doesn't have to be me."

It doesn't have to be me.

Seated people love the success of others; they rejoice that this beautiful thing happened, and it didn't have to be through them. God has a specific and glorious plan for the good works He has prepared in advance for you to do. They are exactly right for you. When others advance in the directions of their dreams, and you feel left behind, anonymous, and unproductive, remember that you are seated at the table, abiding in Christ, awaiting your instructions.

Am I still a high-achieving woman? Yes. Am I still driven and productive and thrilled when I check off another goal from my ever-growing checklist? Yes. Am I still recognized at work? Yes. I'm still a hard worker who loves to achieve, but I am learning to do this work out of an overflow of intimacy with Jesus. I don't work to please anyone, to gain importance, or to win any recognition.

I'm at the table already. I'm learning that, at this table, if God invites me to live a hidden life, with no recognition, no cameras, no attention, and no awards, I could agree to live that life. My heart fills with peace and joy when I realize just how free I'm becoming.

We can stop working so hard for our seat through our achievements. We are already at the table.

SIT AND SAVOR

Read John 15.

1. Embracing irrelevance, becoming anonymous, and ceasing to be remarkable go against our cultural upbringing. What fears do you have when you read the words *irrelevant, anonymous, unremarkable*? Why is it so hard to think about these words being true to any extent in our lives?

2. Can a person who is seated in Christ still be driven to achieve? Are high-achievers not living as seated at the royal table? Why or why not?

3. How would your work change if you knew you had already won the greatest prize, the most recognition, and the highest honor? What would now motivate you to do your best each day?

4. What does it mean to you to "abide in Christ"? How do you know you're abiding? How would you advise others if they asked, "How do I abide in Christ?"

5. Discuss with the group or journal on your own what it means that "together" we bear fruit for God's kingdom.

PART THREE

SEATED AND
SURRENDERED

—

CHAPTER 8

FOUR HARD
BUT GREAT QUESTIONS

Therefore, I urge you, brothers and sisters, in view of God's mercy,
to offer your bodies as a living sacrifice, holy and pleasing to
God—this is your true and proper worship. Do not conform to
the pattern of this world, but be transformed by the renewing
of your mind. Then you will be able to test and approve what
God's will is—his good, pleasing and perfect will.

—ROMANS 12:1–2

When we're seated in Christ in the heavenly realms, we're in the safest, most secure spot to do the beautiful and God-directed work of caring for our souls.

At no time is our seat threatened. At no time will someone come and swipe the seat from under us. Imagine yourself at the table next to Jesus. His arm is around you and you look at each other.

You're *adoring* instead of agonizing over your appearance.

You're *accessing* instead of architecting your life around affluence.

You're *abiding* instead of achieving.

Now what?

Are you ready to stop, take a deep breath, and ask yourself a few simple questions? A great question, like a stabilizing beam in a building, can reorient a person faster than any other rhetorical tool. A great question can cut to the heart. It can expose us and shine truth into the innermost place.

God often uses a great question to set the soul free.

—✳—

I like to assign students "The Doctor," a short story by Andre Dubus.[1] A doctor comes upon a little boy who has fallen into a creek and becomes trapped under a stone slab that has broken off the bridge above him, pinning the child under a few inches of water. The doctor does everything he can to remove the stone slab, but cannot. He runs up a hill to a nearby house for assistance.

Eventually, the boy drowns, and it takes several strong men to lift the stone off his chest. Days later, the doctor, who couldn't believe his failure, figured out how he might have saved the boy. He recalls that by a house near the creek, a green garden hose lay on the lawn. Had he taken his pocketknife and cut a length of hose, he might have put it into the boy's mouth, like a snorkel, so he could breathe until help came to remove the stone slab.

I tell my students that the doctor failed because he asked the wrong question. He misunderstood the problem. The question should not have been, "How can I get this stone off the boy?" but "How can I get this boy to *breathe*?" Had the doctor asked the right question, he might have saved a life that day.

We feel the weight of our circumstances—that stone slab of

THERE'S SOMETHING ABOUT A GOOD QUESTION THAT CUTS TO THE HEART AND BECKONS THE TRUTH.

whatever pain we're in—and we beg God to just give us a new seat. But our circumstances aren't the real problem. The problem is we *need to breathe.* We need more of Jesus. We need the Holy Spirit to remind us that we are seated in Christ and completely seen, secure, and satisfied.

There's something about a good question that cuts to the heart and beckons the truth.

I tell my students that if we ask the wrong questions in a crisis, we'll get the wrong answer. The right questions get to the heart of a matter, primary causes, root issues. Remember the boy's primary problem: *not* that he had a stone on him, but that he couldn't breathe.

The right question can save a life.

I discovered four hard but great questions that I wrote in my journal to help me find a way to breathe on my most difficult days. I visualize my seat with Jesus in the heavenly realms, and then I ask the following:

1. *Is knowing Jesus better than anything?*
2. *Will I live the life God asks me to?*
3. *Is there anything in my life that doesn't please God?*
4. *Am I available to be God's spokesperson?*

Do I have the faith to answer these questions honestly? Can I answer them in ways that are right and good and biblical? What will happen to me if I don't? I know, deep within, my life would change based on how I answer these questions. I either move into despair and greater striving for a seat at the next table, or I move into the peace that passes all understanding and the joy that awaits the surrendered heart. These four questions penetrate into the locked areas of secret sin. The questions address the matter of whom I would worship, whom I would obey, what I would value, and what purpose my life would assume.

You can be honest with God right now. You are safe. You are loved. You are secure. You can ask hard questions because at no time is your relationship with Jesus threatened. He loves you and is with you. Scripture is clear: Nothing can snatch you out of His hand (see John 10:29). Further, Ephesians 2:6 says that God "raised us up *with* Christ and seated us *with* him in the heavenly realms *in* Christ Jesus" (emphasis mine). Notice these prepositions—we are seated "with him" but also, astonishingly, "in" Christ Jesus. We are "in the interior of some whole" in this case, Jesus Christ. We are "in."

We are in.

We are *in* Christ Jesus, and He is seated in a place of honor and authority.

Why does this matter? It matters because if we're going to be honest with ourselves and with God—and if we want to expose idols and sin in our lives—we need to know we are in a place of unconditional acceptance and love. We need to know that we will not live in shame or rejection when we go to Jesus with our sin and doubt and anger and despair.

We need to know that we are seated.

—⁂—

I stared at the questions.

As I started taking notes, something clicked into place the way a camera lens clicks into focus. Something changed in me when I asked myself these four questions.

QUESTION ONE

Is knowing Jesus better than anything?

Scripture contains several dozen "better than" statements. What's better than fame? What's better than wealth? What's better than even life itself?

I think about what I believe is "better than" being with Jesus. When I'm seated in Christ, I begin to believe that knowing Jesus and being with Him is better than any life I could design or even imagine for myself. Should I say that again?

Knowing Jesus and being with Him is better than any life I could design or imagine for myself.

What's the very best life you could imagine for yourself? Marriage and children? Houses? A prestigious or meaningful career? Beauty? Fame? Wealth?

Is knowing Jesus better than any of these? And by "better," I mean this: Is knowing Jesus more pleasurable, more exciting, more satisfying, more meaningful, more purposeful, and more full than *anything* I have or hope to possess? Can I really say that?

I think this question saved my life. It continues to save my life.

If the answer is no, then I'm going to continue to struggle. Jesus must have not been telling the truth when He promised life "to the full" (John 10:10), or that "rivers of living water will flow from within" (John 7:38). He must have been confused when He suggested that it would be foolish for me to "gain the whole world, yet forfeit [my] soul" (Mark 8:36). And Paul, proclaiming the truth of God, must have been out of his mind when he said in Philippians 3:7–8:

> But whatever were gains to me I now consider loss for the sake
> of Christ. What is more, I consider everything a loss because

of the surpassing worth of knowing Christ Jesus my Lord, for whose sake I have lost all things.

Did Paul honestly believe that knowing Christ Jesus was better than "all things"?

To know Christ—that was what excited Paul. That was what he dreamed about for himself. And for others? What did he dream for other Christians? He modeled a beautiful prayer for us in Ephesians 1:17: "I keep asking that the God of our Lord Jesus Christ, the glorious Father, may give you the Spirit of wisdom and revelation, so that you may know him better."

Knowing and enjoying Jesus is the point of the Christian life, and when I lose this essential truth, I'm doomed to a life of forever chasing after the next dream. I will continually compare my life to that of others, imagining their happiness and their joy, while bemoaning my own situation.

If the answer to the question "Is knowing Jesus better than anything?" is no, then why bother with worshiping that kind of God?

LORD, HELP ME EMPTY MY HANDS OF THE JUNK AND RECEIVE ALL OF YOU.

If knowing Jesus isn't enough, then of course we might turn to whatever does promise satisfaction.

I've lived long enough to know that what we pursue apart from Jesus does not satisfy. I've also lived long enough to know the kind of mental lists we make about what we imagine will bring us happiness. We think, "If only this were different." God might be enough for us if this one thing changed. Some people will think such specific "if onlys" as:

1. If only I owned _____ (fill in the possession)

2. If only I had _____ to love me (fill in the name of the person)

3. If only I could _____ (fill in the accomplishment)

4. If only I lived _____ (fill in the location)

5. If only I looked like _____ (fill in the dream body, face, or wardrobe)

6. If only I had a purpose like _____ (fill in the area of influence you desire)

7. If only I could raise _____ (fill in the type of family you imagine)

8. If only I could master _____ (fill in the skill you want to learn)

9. If only I could experience _____ (fill in the adventure you long for)

10. If only people would see me as _____ (fill in what you expect others to think of you)

The problem with "if onlys" is that they don't deliver what they promise. Truly, they don't. My fight to want more didn't end when I earned my PhD, published, married, and had children. The if onlys continued, imprisoning me in discontentment and longing. They did not ever provide the unfailing love, acceptance, and joy that comes in the presence of Jesus. They don't ever provide the well-being and the *shalom* peace of completeness and absolute contentment (Psalm 29:11; Psalm 85:8) in the presence of the Prince of Peace. The women I know who've changed jobs, husbands, noses, and cities still suffer inside. The women I know who've earned PhDs, published books, traveled extensively, achieved fitness goals, or amassed wealth still want more.

Eve was in paradise, and yet, she could be tempted by an "if only." That brings me some comfort because if even in paradise, Eve was enamored with an "if only," then I can be sure that regardless of my circumstances, I'm not alone in the power of the "if only" temptation that slithers into my own heart.

The first question is my weapon against the "if only": Is knowing Jesus better than anything?

Yes. Yes it is.

But how can I believe it? I asked God to help me believe it. I asked for the faith to believe it. I asked God to help me to know Him—not primarily as my provider or the One who blesses me (although He does both), but as my Lord, the almighty God. I asked God to help me worship Him like this.

I think of worshiping Jesus from my seat in the heavenly realms, sometimes every few minutes if I must. And sometimes, God sends someone with a childlike heart to remind me what it means to know Jesus like this. A few weeks ago, my daughters and I explored the Hayden Planetarium's Digital Universe that combines data from all over the world to provide the most comprehensive video of the observable universe. I play the video, and we sit there, mouths agape, as we observe quasars (the farthest objects scientists can detect) amid all the known galaxies in the universe. I turn to my daughters, overwhelmed with the sublime experience of it, and I say, "I cannot wait to get to heaven so I can ask God all about this. I have so many questions about the universe!"

My younger daughter looks at me as if I am absolutely crazy, like I have completely lost my mind. She says, "Mom, none of this will matter because you will be with Jesus."

I will be with Jesus. I *am* with Jesus. In my seat in the heavenly realms, I worship this God who set me free. Knowing this God is better than anything—even all the knowledge of the mysteries of the universe.

In my seat, I have asked God—and continue to ask Him—to help me understand my seat in the heavenly realms. I want to receive all of Jesus. Not receive His gifts, but receive Him. I need to empty my hands of the junk I want and receive what Jesus has. As I think about my seat in the heavenly realms, I can say this to Jesus:

Lord, help me to empty my hands and receive all of You.

Knowing You is better than anything else. I turn away from these idols, my "if onlys," and I pray that You help me to find fullness in You alone.

—ɷ—

With that first question decided in my heart—that knowing Jesus was better than anything—the "if onlys" scattered like dandelion seeds in the summer breeze. I experienced peace and contentment because intimacy with Jesus drew me out of my circumstances and provided that green garden hose so I could breathe. But a second question stared back at me from my journal:

QUESTION TWO
Will I live the life God asks me to?

When I'm struggling with wanting a different life—or if I hear any tempting siren song luring me to a different seat at another table, I ask myself this question: Will I live the life God asks me to?

Will I? Even if it means I'm *ugly*? Even if it means I'm *anonymous* with no achievement or prestige? Even if it means I'm *poor*?"

Even if . . .

I pause. I'm debating with myself. I'm listing out every "even if" I can imagine. I see that false self staring back at me. Could I say to Jesus in that moment that He has the right to do whatever He wants to do with my life because it belongs to Him? Even if it meant suffering or loss or pain? Even if it meant giving up everything? Could I move that deeply into a truly surrendered life? What would I have to believe is true about God in order to do this?

Does He love me? Does He want the best for me? Can I trust Him? I know myself: I cling to my own life, my own plans, and my ideas of what happiness looks like. I don't know how, like Paul, "[to be] crucified with Christ" (Galatians 2:20). I don't know how to "[lose] [my] life" to find it (Matthew 16:25). The question, "Will I live the life God asks me to?" however, sets me on the path to surrender.

By faith, and with the power of the Holy Spirit, I cry out, "Yes, Lord!"

When I agree to live the life God asks me to, I can breathe again. I'm the little boy with the stone on his chest who finally finds the green garden hose.

You may have your own "even ifs." Right now, you might fear that following Jesus wholeheartedly and allowing Him to direct your life will mean suffering or loss. You might doubt God's power or goodness. You might struggle with whether or not God could protect your life, guard your dreams, and care for you and your loved ones.

I struggle with the same fears.

I sit at the table with Jesus and I gaze at Him. I choose to believe in His love and goodness. I choose to believe in His power. I consider everything I know about Him—His love, His power, His goodness, His authority, His sovereignty, His holiness, His wisdom, and His mercy, and *I offer myself* as a "living sacrifice, holy and pleasing to God" (Romans 12:1). I see the truth of Colossians 3:3–4 where Paul writes, "you died, and your life is now hidden with Christ in God. When Christ, who is your life, appears, then you also will appear with him in glory."

Christ is now my life. I'm born again as a "new creation" (2 Corinthians 5:17). I let myself be crucified with Christ; I'm now sanctified into a new kind of beautiful death of self, a holy death unto the Lord. Here, I surrender my life to Christ and let Him control and direct everything. I tell Jesus everything—all the "even if" fears—and I tell Him that He owns my life because I am "bought at a price" (1 Corinthians 6:20) of His shed blood.

I offer myself.

I will live the life God asks me to. It's a declaration of my will and an attitude of my heart and mind to live in surrender. It's a precious and profound death of self that cracks the shell so the real, true me can emerge. When I'm poised in this place—knowing that Jesus is better than anything and that I'm willing to live the life God asks me to—I begin to consider my life from the perspective of personal holiness. I stay seated with Christ in the heavenly realms, and I ask the next question:

QUESTION THREE
"Is there anything in my life that doesn't please God?"

This question helps me daily as we're told in Galatians to "keep in step with the Spirit" (Galatians 5:25). When I'm choosing to live according to my "flesh," I'm choosing thoughts and activities that do not please God. In Romans we're told that the "mind governed by the Spirit is life and peace" but that "the mind governed by the flesh is death" (Romans 8:6). I know that I can hardly trust my own ways as described in Proverbs 14:12 where even the wisest king wrote, "There is a way that appears to be right, but in the end it leads to death."

I know my capacity for self-deception and going my own independent way. I know that there's a part of me—my flesh—that desires things contrary to God's ways. As I meditate on Galatians 5:16–25, for example, I see examples of the acts of the sinful nature that still dwell inside of me.

As we grow in maturity in Christ, we're able to more and more keep in step with the Spirit and turn from the flesh by the Holy Spirit's power. But at no time are we living under condemnation.

In my early twenties, I lived under so much guilt and condemnation for the sinful choices I made though I was a believer. I was clearly—in many forms—living out the acts of my flesh. I could recite 1 John 1:9: "If we confess our sins, he is faithful and just and will forgive us our sins and purify us from all unrighteousness," but when I asked Jesus to forgive me, I didn't really know how to experience that love and forgiveness. I often quoted Romans 8:1 to myself that "there is now no condemnation for those who are in Christ Jesus." Over and over again, I mentally repeated this truth.

When we're seated with Christ, the difference is that Jesus is with us, and we are looking at our sin together. He is giving us power to change. He isn't shaking His finger or turning His face away when we come to Him with a repentant heart. He's ready to embrace us in the midst of our sin. He loves me. He loves you. He delights in us. We are seated in this delight and acceptance.

The question "Is there anything in my life that doesn't please God?" is one designed to cleanse the heart and help us deeply abide with Jesus. Since I know my sin grieves the Holy Spirit (Ephesians 4:30) and that it harms my sweet intimacy with Jesus (Psalm 66:18), I carefully consider my attitudes and behaviors. I'm also aware that sin brings "trouble and distress" into my life (Romans 2:9), so I'm eager to examine my heart for any areas of sin.

We know that, although we are saved from the punishment of sin and that our sins are not held against us, we still battle the sin nature within us. But Christ sympathizes with us in our struggle with sin (Hebrews 4:15). I am seated in Christ, together with all the saints and with a God who understands, and now I can examine my life to grow into godliness.

Growing in godliness, however, requires knowledge of the ancient paths that God lays out. He designs life to work best within certain parameters, but many people do not know what these boundaries are. They don't know how to live uprightly because the culture has so diluted what it means to live a godly life. We need help to understand these paths.

Consider this wonderful promise from Isaiah 48:17: "I am the Lord your God, who teaches you what is best for you, who directs you in the way you should go."

When I ask myself, "Is there anything in my life that doesn't please God?" I'm asking God to show me what is best and to lead me into the right kind of living. I want a life "filled with the fruit of righteousness that comes through Jesus Christ" (Philippians 1:11).

So I examine my life carefully and pray as David did:

Search me, God, and know my heart; test me and know my anxious thoughts. See if there is any offensive way in me, and lead me in the way everlasting. (Psalm 139:23–24)

All day long, we're assaulted with different messages from the media and culture that can distract us from God's best ways. A few years ago, I compiled a list of ten questions to help me, like Paul prays, "to discern what is best" (Philippians 1:10).

I want to know "what is best." Here are some questions that guide my life even today:

1. Does this activity bring me closer to Jesus or farther away?
2. Is this activity against the law or another authority?
3. Is this activity forbidden in Scripture?
4. Does this activity help others know Jesus?
5. Would I be embarrassed if Jesus arrived and saw me doing this thing?
6. Is this decision more likely to bring me into temptation or into godly choices?
7. Do people I respect and admire agree with this activity?
8. Does this activity bring me under its power where I can't control myself?
9. How do I feel about myself and my relationship with God after doing this thing or being with this person?
10. Is the Holy Spirit saying no, and am I ignoring Him?

I've turned off certain movies, closed certain books, ended various dating relationships, took different jobs, stopped certain addictive behaviors, and even moved because of these questions. I hope they help you as you begin to make godly choices for your life.

As we grow as Christians and learn to make these good choices, we must remember that we are always accepted and loved by Jesus. To help direct my soul into these truths, I remember the day a mentor asked me, "How do you think God feels about you right now?" At the time, I said—like so many of us

> MY MOTIVATION ISN'T TO PLEASE GOD OR TO EARN HIS FAVOR; THAT'S ALREADY DECIDED. MY MOTIVATION IS TO *ENJOY* JESUS MORE AND MORE.

might—that Jesus was surely embarrassed, disappointed, and sad about me. Not true! I learned to take those condemning lies and say, "I know that Jesus is absolutely delighted by me. I am His chosen princess at the royal table."

If you ask women what God feels about them, I highly doubt you'll receive this kind of answer from many. So many of us believe Jesus doesn't really love us. We imagine a frowning, angry, and disappointed face when we think of Jesus. When did we start imagining Jesus as disappointed and ashamed of us? I began to wonder if we lose the truth as we age, so I asked a small child—my own daughter—the question.

I asked my younger daughter, "How do you think Jesus feels about you?"

She smiled and her eyes lit up as she answered quickly and without a bit of hesitation, "Oh, He is so happy about me!"

We need to recapture the little girl inside us who knows Jesus is so happy about us.

Because I'm seated in Christ, when I look at the ways I must change, I don't feel condemned. I feel *excited to grow*. I feel thrilled that Jesus would continue to refine and shape me into His image.

When I first began asking God the question, "Is there anything in my life that doesn't please You?" the answers were obvious. I knew that many things about my life went against God's word. I felt the deep conviction of the Holy Spirit about various behaviors and attitudes. I confessed those things, and I began to avoid places and people that encouraged me to compromise. I learned to sow to "please the spirit" instead of my flesh.

I read in Galatians 6:8 that "Whoever sows to please their flesh, from the flesh will reap destruction; whoever sows to please the Spirit, from the Spirit will reap eternal life." Sowing to please the Spirit meant doing things that helped develop the parts of my life that were God-honoring. It meant spending time in prayer and Bible study. It meant connecting with like-minded people. It meant finding mentors who could help me grow and hold me accountable for temptation areas of my life. I learned to stop doing things that were "sowing to please my flesh" including certain books, movies, parties, and communities that only pushed me away from God. I didn't want anything to come between Jesus and me. I wanted, like David prayed in Psalm 86:11, "an undivided heart" so I could praise God and walk closely with Him.

But is it worth it? Is a godly life that great that it outweighs the pleasures of sin? I will tell you this: Nothing—nothing!—compares with the peace of the Holy Spirit and knowing you are experiencing a close relationship with Jesus. Anything that would hinder you from God's ways is a temporary happiness that will eventually reveal itself for what it is.

Think of Paul's great question in Romans 6:21: "What benefit did you reap at that time from the things you are now ashamed of? Those things result in death!" When I look back on my life, I can tell you that sin offers no benefit. It only brings pain and suffering and loss and shame. But the times I spent journaling my thoughts to Jesus, praying, and studying my Bible? Those times have generated more wisdom, fruit, and well-being than you can imagine. God's word, as it says in 1 Thessalonians 2:13 continues to "work in you who believe." God's word will work within me to lead me away from sin and toward godliness.

Today, I love asking Jesus, "Is there anything in my life that doesn't please You?" This is a joyful, not condemning or depressing process. I'm seated in Christ, covered by Christ's righteousness, and fully accepted. Therefore, the reason I aim to live a godly life isn't out of a "works" mentality or any kind of legalism. It's because I want to continue to allow God to shape me into a woman who's more and more like Jesus. My motivation isn't to please God or to earn His favor; that's already decided. My motivation is to *enjoy* Jesus more and more and to allow His Holy Spirit to lead me into deeper freedom and intimacy with Jesus.

—ɷ—

Once I sit there at the table in the heavenly realms, knowing that Jesus is better than anything, that I will live the life God asks me to, and that I will turn from things in my life that don't please God, I'm primed for the next and final question:

QUESTION FOUR
Am I available to be God's spokesperson?

Agreeing with God that I might make myself available to proclaim His name—to speak on His behalf to others—transformed the purpose of my ordinary days. It meant rethinking my time. It meant praying about my schedule. It meant opening up space in my life for the purpose of being available to love and serve others. The word "available" means to be used at someone else's disposal.

It means being ready for use *at any time.*

Seated people, like the Knights of the Round Table, are available at any time to serve King Arthur. Nothing else takes priority over this. They never say, "I'm sorry, but I'm busy. Go ask someone else." I want to be like Isaiah who, when God asked, "Whom shall I send?" replied, "Here I am. Send me" (Isaiah 6:8). I want to be like Paul whose advice to young Timothy was to "be prepared in season and out of season" to preach the word. Paul was ready at all times, and in Colossians 4:3, he prays that "God may open a door" for the message of the gospel. Every circumstance was about proclaiming the gospel.

Was I available to be God's spokesperson? Like Paul? Like the apostles? Was I as eager and unashamed as that? And what did it mean to clear my schedule and to make myself available?

I answered this question with "Yes." I put aside my frantic and fame-seeking life to simply be available. I didn't even know what that meant, really. I just know that I agreed to be available to the Lord to be His spokesperson, and what followed next changed me in ways I had never imagined.

SIT AND SAVOR

Read Psalm 63:3.

1. Is knowing Jesus better than anything—even life itself? List out all the things that tempt you as better than knowing Jesus.

2. Will you live the life God asks you to? Jot down the "even if" statements that immediately come to mind.

3. Is there anything in your life that doesn't please God? Prayerfully examine your life, confess, and repent (1 John 1:9).

4. What thoughts come to mind when you think about being a "spokesperson"?

5. Are you available to be God's spokesperson? What would keep you from being available?

PART FOUR

SEATED AND SENT

—◊—

CHAPTER 9

AVAILABLE LIVING

Beware the barrenness of a busy life.

—SOCRATES

A strange and beautiful journey began for me when I told God I was available.

Not just any kind of available. I was going to be available to proclaim Jesus wherever, whenever, and however God led me.

I said, "I am available to be your spokesperson, Jesus. Use me. Bring me to people, or bring people to me, and I will love them, pray for them, and tell them about You."

At the time, I wondered if God might instead send me to Africa like my professor friends down the street. I wondered if I could go to the Haitian orphans or the Dominican Republic like those in my church. I was ready to suffer and sacrifice. I imagined I might *glamorously suffer* and post all the pictures of my sacrifices in developing countries on social media.

Even in my godly conviction to serve others, the poison of self-promotion and self-importance still clung to me like barnacles on a ship. I didn't understand how to live a seated life and move into serving others where my service wasn't ultimately about me.

I was like the once demon-possessed man who was ready to follow Jesus anywhere. I was ready to get into the boat with Jesus and *glamorously* and *publically* suffer. This was just another seat I longed for, but God knew how to heal my heart.

We read the story:

> As Jesus was getting into the boat, the man who had been demon possessed begged to go with him. But Jesus said, "No, go home to your family, and tell them everything the Lord has done for you and how merciful he has been." So the man started off to visit the Ten Towns of that region and began to proclaim the great things Jesus had done for him; and everyone was amazed at what he told them. (Mark 5:18–20 NLT)

I wanted excitement and high-impact kind of mission work, just like the healed man in the account, but here I was, shoved out of the boat and sent back to my plain old neighborhood. I wanted to make a name for myself back then, but slowly, through Ephesians 2:6, I realized being available meant a willingness to follow God's leading into specific tasks—whether unseen or public, ordinary or magnificent. Instead of a glamorous life I had always sought—and sometimes lived—my life suddenly became *very small*.

I chose to accept instructions from God to love my neighbors (Matthew 22:39) in ordinary, simple, and daily ways.

As I spent time with the Lord and pondered this new assignment to love and bless my neighbors, I read the claim in Acts 17:26 that God had "marked out [my] appointed times in history and the boundaries of [my] lands." Some translations say that God "searches out the exact places" where we live. He did this so people "would seek him and perhaps reach out for him and find him, though he is not far from any one of us."

My husband and I talked about how the reason people can

reach out and find Jesus, the reason why He is not far from them, is because Jesus is here *through us*. He chose for me to live on this street, to teach in this department on campus, and to walk where I walk. Sure, it did seem narrow and small in scope, but I trusted the promise in Psalm 16:6 that the "boundary lines have fallen for me in pleasant places."

WHAT WOULD IT MEAN TO LOVE AND SERVE THESE NEIGHBORS AND LEARN ABOUT THEIR LIVES— THE ATHEIST, BUDDHIST, UNIVERSALIST, AND NEW AGE NEIGHBORS?

I thought of the one-mile radius of my neighborhood—the boundaries of my lands. What would happen if I exclusively devoted myself to these people within walking distance from my home? I would live within a narrow boundary of three streets and love *these* neighbors. I would do this as the days turned into months and the months turned into years.

My mission: to live in community with my neighbors. How would I? What would it involve? What did it mean to make oneself exclusively devoted—exclusively available—to the neighbors? And could I make myself vulnerable to them and open my heart to be blessed and served in return? What would it mean to love and serve these neighbors and learn about their lives—the atheist, Buddhist, universalist, and New Age neighbors? What would I experience as I learned from the practicing yogi or the various spiritual practices—as diverse as you can imagine—of those on my street alone? How could I best serve the families going through divorce, illness, or grief?

I debated with myself: *It's so much easier just to serve at church.*

I could teach Sunday school or lead a Bible study. I could hang out with Christian women and enjoy community with them. I could start prayer groups with all my Christian friends. I'll do anything—anything but love my neighbor! If I truly made myself available to the people God has placed in my life—neighbors, coworkers, and students—what about *me*? What about my glamorous life full of fame and fortune? Loving my neighbor wasn't in my plan to succeed and "be somebody."

What I've slowly learned in the last eight years crystalized with this assignment. What I read in Ephesians 2:6 was this: *I'm seated in Christ. I don't need to be "somebody" anymore.* Besides, when I'm seated in Christ, I have energy for other people because I'm not exhausting myself trying to earn a spot through appearance, affluence, and achievement. I'm sitting down with Jesus and making myself available.

It was a secret little life, tucked inside a rented house in a tree-lined neighborhood in Central Pennsylvania. Unannounced to the rest of the world, our family began to gather the neighbors together in specific ways. We did these things because we sensed God wanted us to intentionally love our neighbors and be available.

I wasn't going to be famous. I wasn't going to be rich.

It wasn't going to be glamorous.

But it would be *glorious.*

It would be beautifully, mysteriously, wonderfully, and peacefully ordinary but *supernatural.* And supernatural living made this knight of the Round Table wake up with joy in anticipation with what God would do next.

Before I share the details, I want to pass on a simple passage that began to govern each day. In Philippians 1:25–26, Paul expresses the desire of his heart for what it means to spend time with people. He says, "I will continue with all of you for your progress and joy in the faith, so that through my being with you again your boasting in Christ Jesus will abound on account of me."

In other words, as we spend time with others, we aim to build their faith, bring joy to them, and cause an overflowing sense of glorying in, or boasting about, Jesus. With this mission in mind, I began to trust God with my availability to others.

—w—

On the first day I decided to declare my availability to Jesus, I began to decline fancy lunches and outings across town; I restrained myself from shopping trips; I disappointed countless people who wanted me to do various things (speak, write, teach, lead); I decided to clear my schedule of morning Bible studies and mothers' groups at my church. I burrowed deeply into my neighborhood that first week.

I stayed home. Anonymous. Ordinary. Unscheduled.

I prayed about my "natural pathways" and how to say no to offers that took me away from where God had naturally and clearly placed me. I knew I lived in a neighborhood, served in ministry to graduate students, and taught a few classes of Penn State students. In the quiet of my heart and soul as I read my Bible and prayed, I felt that gentle whisper of God's Holy Spirit. *Right here. I've put you right here.* I realized just how scattered my life had become. What would it look like to gather my life in and focus on one clear, simple mission? To scatter means to disperse in different directions. When we're scattered, it means we're investing energy in multiple, often opposing directions.

The opposite of scatter is to *gather in.*

I considered the difference between a scattered life and a life that's gathered in. Before that morning in my rocking chair, I had been frazzled every single day. I was involved in four major campus projects including teaching three different courses and directing an unrelated project for another program. Besides this, I was freelance writing, meeting with graduate students, parenting, trying to be a great wife, serving my church, relating superficially to neighbors, and attempting to keep a clean house while preparing nutritious meals. And exercising. And remembering to do the laundry.

I often lost my temper with my family. I was angry and very, very moody.

I needed to gather my life in. What would happen if I directed all my energy in one direction and not ten? I knew I would love the neighbors, that was clear, but what about my professional life? I gathered in by requesting from my department that I only teach the same course each semester (instead of two or three different kinds), and I could focus my energy on making that one course great and then teach it multiple times. I directed my freelance writing projects to relate to my course work. I declined directing programs that didn't relate to this one course. I reduced my professional life to one natural pathway, and I developed it with flair.

A SCATTERED LIFE, DIFFUSED AND DIMINISHED OF POWER, ISN'T A FUN LIFE TO LIVE. A GATHERED LIFE FEELS SIMPLE AND ENERGIZED.

I focused on verbs—in my writing class and in my relationship with Jesus. Verbs. Verbs like *seated*.

After all, being available meant I had to stop doing things to make space. Gathering in allowed for this space. It increased my energy and my capacity to be fully present and refreshed each day.

Gathering in made me narrow my scope to my neighbors, my one course, our weekly meeting with graduate students, and my family. I said no to everything else by God's leading and power.

A scattered life, diffused and diminished of power, isn't a fun life to live. It's a tired life, a moody life, a life that feels spent before noon. A gathered life feels simple and energized. There's time to reflect, learn a dance, cook a gourmet meal, and keep a blog. There's time to drink coffee with a neighbor, hunt for a turtle in your backyard, or make homemade pizza with a child. There's time to stay in your seat in the heavenly realms and worship Jesus.

I told my wise neighbor April Yorke how I was trusting God for this. She told me her secret for sanity in the midst of pursuing a PhD, raising young children, maintaining a great marriage, and hosting neighborhood events.

"I live at 60 percent."

"What do you mean?" I turned to her, curious and confused.

"Some women live their lives at 90 percent capacity. They are already nearly at their energy expenditure limit each day. So when a new stressor adds into the mix, they explode. They go ballistic. They're atomic bombs that go off in their own homes."

"That was me last night," I confessed. The tiniest comment from a child set me off into tears.

"But if you live at 60 percent of your energy capacity, you're ensuring you have a buffer for emergencies and any changes. You're able to deal with life as it happens. You have reserves."

She walks on, smooth and carefree, while I'm chasing after her to learn more.

"How do you live at 60 percent? What's the secret?"

"Well, I was chronically ill for six years, so I know how to ask myself what I have to offer energy-wise each day. Then, I do *even less* to protect myself from what might come. I say no a lot. And I know when I need to reenergize."

She lives *less* than what she's actually capable of each day. Instead of do *more*, it's do *less*.

I live at 99 percent—nearly maxed out, wild, multitasking, overproducing, checking-off-my-to-do-list kind of living. April reminds me that this 60 percent rule applies not only to time and energy, but also our emotional and financial resources. She further adds that this way of living changes everything. She says, "It forces me to focus on what I feel is most important, what I truly value in life, rather than running around trying to do everything."

I wanted to live at 60 percent. I needed to live at 60 percent. I think I needed to slow my own children down as well.

I don't want to snap at my family because I have no reserves. I don't want to raise my voice because I'm maxed out. I don't want to fret when the car needs repair, if dinner burns, or if a supervisor gives me a new assignment.

The birds know this. I checked the nest outside the window, and the robin has stopped laying eggs. The nest, with four gorgeous eggs, is *at capacity*. Natural processes tend to stick within their boundaries. Animals rarely do too much on purpose.

I'll be honest: When I felt God leading me to make myself available to my own neighborhood and to do less, I said, "Oh God, no! Don't make me live small. I want big and glamorous! I'm supposed to be in a big city with my name in lights!" Instead, I opened up my front door, and when the wind blew, I could smell the horse manure from the farms around my county. *Really, Jesus? Horse poop? I want fame and glory and You give me manure?* (By the way, as you know, manure is fertilizer. It makes things grow into the best they can be.)

—⚮—

I sat on the couch with my Bible and journal. I sipped from a cup of coffee with hazelnut creamer. This was my first morning of availability. I canceled everything. I felt under specific orders from Jesus to stay home and *be available*. It felt crazy. It felt wasteful. It felt like a big mistake for extroverted, high-capacity, academically qualified me to sit in my empty house on my old couch in my living room and *do nothing*. I realized with shame that when I'm fighting for a seat at the table, I feel like what makes me important is how busy I am. Seated people don't have to be busy. They live unhurried lives. They live beautifully unhurried lives.

Just as I'm about to abandon this insane commitment to availability, I hear the crunch of tires in my driveway. I peer out of my front window to see a burgundy minivan in the driveway. A gorgeous Italian woman with dark curly hair—she's stunning— pushes open the van door with her trim and muscular leg. She's my neighbor who lives at the end of the street. She's balancing two lattes in her hands as she expertly closes the van door and makes her way to my front porch. She rings the bell with her elbow before I can swing open the door.

"I just got a new haircut," she says, smiling and turning her beautiful face from side to side. "I wanted to show you. I've brought us some coffee, and I wondered if you were busy. Are you busy?"

Am I busy? Ha! Ha, ha ha!

"No, I have nothing to do. Come right on in!"

On that slow morning, my neighbor and I talked about deep, private things. We talked about ways we need to pray for our children. We shared from our hearts—

IT ALL BEGAN WITH A HAIRCUT, TWO LATTES, AND BEING AVAILABLE.

our pain, our joys, and our hopes—as the morning passed and our coffee cups emptied. This woman, from that moment on, became one of my dearest friends. She trained me in the art of being an Italian mama, complete with cooking lessons, parenting lessons, and marriage lessons. She hosted Italian lunches to introduce me to other Italian mamas in the neighborhood. I learned to love Bruce Springsteen's music (New Jersey Italians love Bruce) and cannoli. I learned to prepare a proper antipasto platter with mozzarella, prosciutto, olives, tomatoes, and fresh basil. I learned about pesto and marinara and good olive oil and pasta. I learned to roast peppers, make meatballs correctly, enjoy a good baked ziti and tortellini, and dip almond biscotti in dark roasted coffee. I learned about homemade pizzelles and ravioli. I made eggplant parmigiana.

I learned about passion from her.

It all began with a haircut, two lattes, and being available.

—∞—

It's a warm, sunny afternoon. I'm standing on the front porch. I look to the left, down where two streets intersect, and then I look to the right, up toward where the street rounds a corner and turns into another street.

Silence. Nothing. Not one child is outside. My own children watch television inside, their expressions blank. There's a hollow ache inside of me. I glance again at these houses—all in a row, trimmed and neat—that harbor families I do not know. I cross my arms over my chest and then release the grip to touch my face and run my forefinger over my lips in a gesture that always accompanies my need to really think.

I tap my lip a few times, thinking.

Then, it occurs to me that *this is not really a community of neighbors*. Not yet. But what if it were? What if all the children played outside together? What if the parents drank coffee together and shared their lives together? What if we raised these children together and took care of one another? I saw it then in my mind: dozens of children jumping rope, riding bikes, and playing tag on this street along with parents who connected with each other and devoted their lives to each other.

I raced into the kitchen and frantically dug into the kitchen junk drawer for the elementary school directory. I began dialing the numbers of any family that had children within a one-mile radius of my home.

"Hello! This is Heather Holleman. You might not know who I am, but I'm going to be in our front yard with bikes and jump ropes and chalk tonight after dinner. I would love it if you and your children would come and play for an hour or so. Six-thirty, our front yard. Thank you!" I dialed the next number and then the next number. "Hello, this is Heather Holleman. You don't know me but . . ."

Argentine writer Jorge Luis Borges once claimed this: "Every destiny, however long and complicated, essentially boils down to *a single moment*—the moment when a man knows, once and for all, who he is."[1]

That was my moment—the one on my front porch when I wanted a neighborhood and knew God was calling me to be radically available. It began with that first phone call. That night after dinner, I went in the front yard with my jump ropes and bikes. All of a sudden, I saw them coming. Family after family arrived on the front lawn to play. As the children raced around (with me timing them with my stopwatch for various races; I even coordinated the ancient games of red light/green light and Mother-may-I), the adults shook hands and talked. We decided right then and there to have neighborhood fitness night every week—even every night if we could.

Children who couldn't ride bikes now ride faster than me. Children who never jump roped before can now beat their own best score in double Dutch. When it grew too dark, we moved our fitness time up. When our group became too large, we moved to the school parking lot, and sometimes up to fifty people came to exercise. When it got too cold, we moved our neighborhood fitness group into our basement for Monday night fitness group.

For five years, we met in our basement during the winter for one hour after dinner for dancing, jumping jacks, and whatever fitness activity we could invent. We challenged each other to jump rope one hundred times, do one hundred jumping jacks, and dance for twenty minutes without stopping. The local news came out to cover our neighborhood fitness group.[2] I even have a letter from the White House, signed by Michelle Obama, thanking our neighborhood for our commitment to healthy living.

In the meantime, something happened to our neighborhood. We all wanted a real community that valued well-being. We committed to walking to school together—one mile—every single morning. We bundled up, even in the snow and rain, and walked. On our one hundredth day of walking to school, we made T-shirts and had a party to celebrate our hundred miles. In addition to our walk-to-school campaign, neighbors began to host healthy neighborhood potlucks, and as a community, we began to change our lives. We chose to make each other a priority. Before we knew what was happening, we discovered we had built a neighborhood.

One night, a couple said, "We've lived in our home for four years, and you were the first neighbor to invite us anywhere."

—⟋⟋—

Availability meant devoting myself to our neighbors and actively designing programs to bring us all together. The Holy Spirit gave me boldness, energy, and insight, and God used my natural extroversion and pep to motivate people. Eventually, neighborhood availability had nothing to do with me anymore. I set the ball in motion, and then, together, families began to connect and inspire each other. I thought, at first, that my role was to bless and encourage others, but it was all the neighbors who began to bless and encourage me. Our activities were small in scope but large in our hearts: the walk-to-school campaign brought up to thirty-five neighbors together—parents and children—who commit to walking that one mile to school.

The neighbors have been walking with me for seven years now. I've walked over 2,500 miles with my neighbors. In addition to walking, Ashley and I began hosting pancake breakfasts for the neighbors. We invited several families over every single Saturday to enjoy breakfast. Saturday morning pancakes gathered, at the most, six families. Monday night neighborhood fitness group gathered, at times, fifty neighbors who came out to jump rope, ride bikes, throw Frisbees and footballs, fly kites, and walk in the neighborhood pool parking lot. Besides this, neighbors gathered for creative women's night, movie nights, men's night, and writing groups, all within that one-mile radius. Together, we've accomplished multiple service

WE ARE PEOPLE MEANT TO PARTICIPATE IN EACH OTHER'S LIVES. WE ALSO HAVE A KINGDOM ASSIGNMENT TO PROCLAIM THE GOSPEL TO A HURTING WORLD.

projects for schools, churches, and shelters, and offered support and care for hurting people.

My daily life looks very ordinary and routine to the outsider. Even my own daughters ask me about it sometimes.

"Do you have to do this every day?" My youngest flops down on my caramel-colored bedspread and rolls over onto her stomach. She's asking out of curiosity, not annoyance.

"Yes," I say. "It changes me."

I'm in the same rocking chair where I cradled her in my arms ten years ago. I glance out the window at the weeping cherry and the swirls of an orange and pink sunrise. I drink coffee with hazelnut creamer from a special mug.

It's the same thing every day: coffee, rocking chair, and sunrise. To my right, in a blue wicker basket, I have my essential tools including Hannah Whitall Smith's *God Is Enough*, the green Bible my friend Elizabeth gave me in 1994, my journal, and my favorite pen (the Pilot G-2 ultrafine point).

Then, the ritual—the dance—begins. It's just Jesus and me as I read an entry from *God Is Enough*, underlining and sighing in agreement with her words. I'm talking to Jesus about what I'm feeling, what I'm worried about, and what's coming ahead. I turn to the Psalms and read the next five. I'm asking Jesus to teach me, to change me. I'm asking Jesus to let His word work within me. I find I'm confessing bad attitudes and shedding off the old me like snakeskin.

I remember I'm seated in Christ, and I see myself there in the heavenly realms. The new me comes into view, hazy at first and then fully here. I'm anchored again. I remember who I am. I open my journal and cry out to God in numbered lists about my children and husband. I pray over what's coming in this day. When I close the old journal and the equally worn Bible, I feel emptied out of every dusty thing that settled upon me in the night.

By 8:00 a.m., I'm out the door, walking children to school.

"Do you do this every day?" my colleagues wonder when they realize the time commitment of walking a mile to school every day.

"Yes," I say. "It changes me."

I'm not just walking; I'm composing a symphony with the rhythm of my steps; I'm forging invisible tethers of love to my neighbors that hold me when I'm lost; I'm remembering the beauty and simplicity of children and elementary school.

I'm not just walking.

It was a spring day maybe a few years into our walk-to-school campaign. I left the house once again to gather all the children to walk the mile to school. Parents came out with coffee mugs in hand to walk with me. I was just walking along, talking to some children, when I felt the deepest sense of belonging.

This was my neighborhood. These were my people. The Italian mamas; the little children; the writers; the artists; the Buddhist woodworker; the Mormons who always brought food when I was sick; the Quakers; the New Age friends who talked about Reiki and energy healing and who worshiped Hindu gods; the atheists; the grieving; the brokenhearted; the divorcing; the chemistry professor; the athletes; the Irish neighbors; the stay-at-home dad—too many to count. I loved them. I belonged to them. I even loved all the dogs and the ferrets one family just adopted. I loved them all.

They belonged to me. This one-mile radius was my life.

As a Christian, I've come to understand that the enemy of our souls, Satan, has a primary task: to separate us from God, ourselves, and one another. Satan uses any negative emotion he can to separate us from one another—jealously, pride, judgment, shame. If we learn how to combat these tactics to attach deeply to our neighbors in devoted communities, we reflect the relational aspects of God. We also manifest what is true about us: we are people meant to participate in each other's lives. We also have a kingdom assignment to proclaim the gospel to a hurting world.

Building the neighborhood was as much about friendship and belonging as it was about gospel proclamation, but what I discovered is that the two go hand in hand. Within the small radius of my neighborhood, several people prayed to receive Christ and were baptized at my church. I realize that on a national scale, this represents minuscule growth. Why bother charting it? What if—within a million other one-mile circles—even a few people came to know Jesus? What if those few people took up the challenge to love within the mile next to them? If everyone loved within a mile, I wonder what could happen to the whole world. Could the gospel radiate out, even from the brokenhearted and ordinary among us, and change the world?

IF EVERY STREET IN THE WORLD HAD PEOPLE ON MISSION TO LOVE THEIR NEIGHBORS AND SEE THEM AS A SPECIFIC ASSIGNMENT FROM GOD TO LOVE, PROTECT, AND BELONG TO, HOW WOULD THE WORLD CHANGE?

Yes. Yes it could.

But we often turn away from the brokenhearted and ordinary. We'd rather minister in great (or at least more exciting) ways rather than the ordinary mile. But remember, "God is close to the brokenhearted and saves those who are crushed and spirit" (Psalm 34:18). I thought that if I wanted to be close to where God is, I should go find brokenhearted people and lead them to their seats in the heavenly realms. It does seem perhaps uncomfortable and ordinary, and I know we'd rather have the influential, the strategic, and the powerful.

But I'm seated in Christ. I don't seek influence and power, and now I'm under specific instructions to be available to my community. I often talk to my students about the importance of investing deeply in literal communities. They feel more and more alone even as they move closer to more people technologically. In fact, we've never been more *connected* in our life. Students have thousands of friends on Facebook, thousands of followers on Twitter and Instagram, and thousands of page views on their blogs. In this virtual universe, we're surrounded by virtual people. Yet, as one of my students proclaimed, "Saying the Internet satisfies my need for real community is like saying a picture of a glass of water satisfies my thirst."

We're thirsty for authentic community, and the Internet isn't satisfying.

Yesterday, a group of women met with me and discussed, "Now what needs do we see in our neighborhood? Is anyone hungry, sick, or in need? How can we help? Does anyone need job training? Does anyone need care?"

If every street in the world had people on mission to love their neighbors and see them as a specific assignment from God to love, protect, and belong to, how would the world change?

Ashley taught me a great ministry principle several years ago: do things *with* people, not always just *for* them. We can all make ourselves available and invite other friends and families into what we are *already doing.* Since I was *already walking* my children to school every day, my family launched that walk-to-school campaign that challenged the neighbors to walk the one mile to school and back every single day. Since we were *already having pancakes* on Saturday, we simply invited the neighbors to join us in what we were already doing. Just yesterday, a neighbor and I decided that we would get together as we were grocery shopping. We were already doing it, and that was one way we could be available to each other.

When we're seated in Christ, we believe that our time and schedule belong to God. We are managers and stewards of the time He gives us. When I agreed with God to make myself available to the people He placed in my natural pathways, life became richer, fuller, and more abundant than you can imagine. Recently, two women found me at a bridal shower I attended. They pulled me into the kitchen and said, "We need your advice. We've been so involved in our church and we love all our Bible studies and fellowship groups. But something's not right. Something's missing. We've heard about you and how you live your life. Could you teach us what you know?"

I told them that they were probably like I once was, living a very comfortable but staid Christian life. I said that I suspected they were ready for the adventure of becoming available to love and serve the people in their neighborhoods and workplaces. It wasn't going to be comfortable, I told them. I tucked my hair over my ear and smiled. I thought of the old me who didn't know she was seated in Christ. I thought of all the ways I sought for meaning and joy that left me missing something. I thought of the day I agreed to be available and how I called all those neighbors to jump rope with me.

It wasn't glamorous. It was never glamorous.

It was *glorious.*

SIT AND SAVOR

—ᴍᴍ—

Read Acts 17 and Psalm 18.

1. Think of your natural pathways and the boundary lines. Where do you spend the most time during the day?

2. Make a list of those people in your natural pathways.

3. In what ways might you make yourself available to these people? What would have to change in your schedule?

4. Using the ministry principle "with and not just for," what are some things you could do "with" people in your life and not just "for" them?

5. What are the greatest needs you can identify in your natural pathways? Why do you think God might have personally led you to these people?

———✺———

CHAPTER 10

SEATED AND SENT

We cannot help speaking about what we have seen and heard.
—Peter and John before the Sanhedrin, Acts 4:20

We are therefore Christ's ambassadors, as though
God were making his appeal through us.
—2 Corinthians 5:20

When I think about being seated in Christ—adoring, accessing, abiding—and now ready and truly available to perform the good works He's prepared for me, nothing excites me more than participating with Jesus in leading others to know Him.

Every day now becomes a supernatural adventure as I make myself available to be God's spokesperson. Every conversation now shimmers with possibility and excitement as I converse with the people God places in my path. I think about the eternal weight of it, and I'm filled with wonder that God grants us the privilege of proclaiming His name to others.

Do you remember how King Arthur in the series *Merlin* anoints each knight of the Round Table and says, "You are now part of the most noble army the world has ever known"? When I see myself as part of the battle to win souls, to advance the kingdom of God, and to use my words to bring light to places of darkness, I greet each day battle ready and bold as a lion. It's because I'm seated at the table and sent out.

I'm *seated* and *sent*.

Christians who describe their spiritual lives as boring, unimportant, or confusing might have forgotten that they are seated and sent on the most exciting adventure that exceeds everything they could even conceive of. When Jesus begins to use us for kingdom purposes, we attach to a grander redemptive story that brings us out of our small lives and small ambitions into something glorious and powerful. We are now part of something supernatural.

I remember the earliest days of talking to friends in school about my love of Jesus. I remember dialoging with professors at the University of Virginia about Jesus. I remember defending my faith regularly as a graduate student at the University of Michigan. But it wasn't until I learned three things that evangelism became a daily lifestyle for me.

First, I learned that *sharing Jesus with people is part of our purpose as Christians still on earth.* Second Corinthians 5:20 reminds us that Jesus was "making his appeal through us" to reconcile people to Himself. Paul declares that we are "Christ's ambassadors." I'm seated in Christ and now sent on the great commission assignment to "go into all the world and preach the gospel to all creation" (Mark 16:15). As if this weren't convincing enough of my purpose, I considered how, when Jesus attracts His very first followers, He says, "Come, follow me, . . . and I will send you out to fish for people" (Matthew 4:19). I agreed with Jesus that I was on a kingdom mission.

This I knew: my life purpose was now to proclaim the hope that comes through faith in Christ alone.

The second important piece of information that transformed

my understanding of evangelism was the notion of *power*. I understood that Jesus gives power and wisdom to be a witness for Him; it doesn't originate from or depend upon me. My mentor at the time shared with me Acts 1:8, where Jesus simply says, "You will receive power when the Holy Spirit comes on you; and you will be my witnesses in Jerusalem, and in all Judea and Samaria, and to the ends of the earth."

I will receive power. I will receive power to be a witness.

It was at that time I understood I was indwelt by the Holy Spirit because I had received Christ into my life, and I prayed that the Holy Spirit would control and direct my conversations with others. I invited that power—by faith—to operate within me more and more.

Third, I knew I needed *training* to talk to others about Jesus. The information I needed wasn't complex, obscure, or inaccessible. A child could learn it. I studied a simple gospel presentation and memorized Bible verses about God's love and plan of salvation for us.[1] I spent many months familiarizing myself with Scripture so I might weave it naturally into conversation with others. I took seriously the spiritual discipline of Scripture memory because I wanted my life to be like the one described in Colossians 3:16. Here, Paul writes, "Let the message of Christ dwell among you richly as you teach and admonish one another with all wisdom through psalms, hymns, and songs from the Spirit, singing to God with gratitude in your hearts." I wanted the "message of Christ" to dwell in me through His word, so I could teach others.

To summarize, I needed to

GOD'S WORD IS POWERFUL. IT CHANGES PEOPLE. IT GETS INSIDE OF THEM AND GERMINATES.

know God's *purpose* for me, to appropriate the *power* to proclaim, and to *practice speaking Scripture* to familiarize myself with God's plan of salvation. This last point matters because we know that "faith comes from hearing the message, and the message is heard through the word about Christ" (Romans 10:17). I knew that God's word interacted with the soul, spirit, and mind, and if I could use it in conversation, the Holy Spirit would animate it in personal ways to that individual, as Hebrews 4:12–13 says.

I studied God's Word in order to use it effectively in conversation because I knew it has special power to build faith and reveal truth. I remembered how in 1 Thessalonians 2:13 we are told that the "word of God is alive and active" in people's hearts and minds.

God's Word is powerful. It changes people. It gets inside of them and germinates.

Knowing my purpose, having power, and practicing speaking God's Word from memory created a foundation of a lifestyle of evangelism that began in my twenties and continues to this day. So exciting was the thought of talking to people about Jesus that I often felt like a racehorse stomping before the gate. *Open the gate already! Just send me people, and I will proclaim!* I felt like the psalmist in Psalm 40:5: "Many, Lord my God, are the wonders you have done, the things you planned for us. None can compare with you; were I to speak and tell of your deeds, they would be too many to declare." I was the writer crying out in Psalm 51:15, "Open my lips, Lord, and my mouth will declare your praise."

I love talking about Jesus. I have so much to declare about Him. I cannot possibly exhaust the list of what to talk about when it comes to Jesus. And believe me, for how much I talk, you would think I'd run out of things to say. For how much I talk about Jesus, you would think I'd annoy my neighbors. But let me tell you this:

Nobody ever told me to stop talking about Jesus. Not once. So I didn't stop.

—⟫⟫—

As I walked children to school with their parents, hosted neighborhood fitness night, served pancakes, and enjoyed Italian mama luncheons, I talked and talked about Jesus. Rather than a sophisticated strategy of winsome, well-articulated theology, I prayed that God would just help me *be myself*. In order to be myself, I acted like the people around me were already Christians. I assumed, as Christians would, that they wanted to hear about Jesus. I assumed, as Christians would, that God was at work in their lives. I assumed, as Christians would, that Jesus was the best thing ever and that hearing about Him delighted their souls.

Believing your audience is open, loving, and eager to learn might be the best evangelism strategy I know because *it works*. And, if you think about it, God *is* at work; Jesus *is* the best thing ever; hearing about Him *will* delight a soul. In my neighborhood, then, I shared what I learned in the Scriptures that morning.

I would say, "I read the coolest thing in Ephesians 2 this morning. Can I tell you?" or "I read something so bizarre in the Bible this morning. I have to tell you." I shared about answered prayer. I would say, "You'll never believe what I prayed for and how God answered." Or even "I am so disappointed and having to really trust God with how He answered this prayer."

I was honest and open. I shared about ongoing spiritual struggles like how to really "be thankful in all circumstances" or how to trust God when my children suffer.[2] I would say, "What do I need to believe about God in order to thank Him when my daughter comes home crying because of a bully? I need to believe He is powerful, good, and in control at all times. What do y'all think about this?"

When neighbors asked me about my day and my writing or speaking projects, I might say, "I'm writing a talk on being seated in Christ. Can I list out my points for you? Tell me if this makes sense."

When I shared the Seated message to one neighbor in the coffee shop, she wasn't offended or annoyed. In fact, she said, "I love it. But I want to know one thing: How do you sustain that feeling of being seated day after day?"

That was her question. She didn't yell at me for talking about Jesus. She didn't tell me I was hyperconservative, narrow-minded, uninformed, or misled. No. She asked a very good question.

Essentially, my speech normalized spiritual conversation and invited others to respond. As I shared from the Scriptures each morning, I often asked neighbors what they thought about certain Bible verses. Sometimes, I might ask them ways I could pray for their families. Remember: Never once, in all my years of living in this neighborhood, has a neighbor said, "I wish you would stop talking about Jesus."

MY YOGI NEIGHBOR ASKED, "CAN WE STILL BE FRIENDS IF I WORSHIP MY GODS AND YOU WORSHIP JESUS CHRIST?"

One morning, I asked my neighbor, one of my dearest friends (a practicing yogi who worshiped various gods, including those from the Hindu faith), if it bothered her that I talked so much about Jesus. I'll never forget what she said: "No! I want to hear everything you have to say about Jesus." When I realized that my neighbors wanted to hear about Jesus, my walk to school became an adventure. Each day, we'd talk more about Jesus. I was so nervous that we'd be rejected when we asked if neighbors wanted to study the Bible, but instead, one of the most resistant neighbors said, "I've been waiting for an invitation like this!"

When we invited the neighbors to study the gospel of John with us over Saturday morning pancakes, I didn't know what would happen. Jesus doesn't mince words in this book. He says quite clearly in John 14:6, "I am the way and the truth and the life. No one comes to the Father except through me." This exclusive claim was the topic of that morning's discussion.

My neighbor promptly told us that she was deeply troubled by Jesus' statement that He is the only way to salvation. "This is so offensive!" she hollered at my husband, Ashley. And then, without skipping a beat, she cried, "I want to hear more. Are we meeting next week?"

Likewise, my yogi neighbor asked, "Can we still be friends if I worship my gods and you worship Jesus Christ?" At first, resistance was great when my neighbors truly understood the gospel. But God began to work in their hearts. Soon, families were joining us in church, finding Bibles to read, and praying to receive Christ. The yogi not only received Christ, but she presented the gospel to her family, baptized her daughter, and led investigative Bible studies of her own on her university campus.

Every day, I'm talking about Jesus, and nobody ever freaks out about it. I'm still learning how to feel seated and sent in my professional life. It's easy to share Christ with my neighbors who accept me, but in my position as a writing instructor, I often wonder how to even identify myself as a Christian. But when I do, I'm always so encouraged. Sometimes, when I simply mention that I'm a Christian as I introduce myself at the beginning of the semester, students immediately engage me in spiritual questions that I can then answer outside of class.

For example, this semester, I introduced myself by saying, "I'm Dr. Holleman, and outside of this class, I help direct a Christian ministry to graduate students and faculty. My Christian faith is very important to me. In fact, part of my professional life is my Christian speaking and writing. I'm fascinated by Greek verbs in Scripture, and I write about them. I'm writing a book on being seated with Christ."

Before I had a chance to catch my breath, a student raised his hand and asked, "How did you choose to be a Christian instead of another religion? I am really thinking about these things. I really want to know."

Every student was staring at me, so I quickly tried to start our writing lesson. But the student who raised his hand asked, "Where does one start reading in the Bible?" The whole class seemed very interested in talking about these things. I asked, "Do you really want to hear about this?" Several students shouted *yes!*

I ended this exchange by saying, "I would love to talk more with any of you about my faith outside of class at a coffee shop."

I witnessed two amazing reminders from that day: students are spiritually searching, and they often look to their professors for answers. Part of being seated and sent means that I can listen to students, answer questions, and direct them to resources to help them on their spiritual journeys when the opportunities arise.

———

Most of my writing and speaking engagement invitations come from groups who truly want to know the "secret" to sharing their faith. I worry that they might leave disappointed in the simplicity of what I share, but by the end, I find audiences feel energy, empowerment, hope, and confidence. Early on in my training in ministry, I learned this definition of successful evangelism: "Success in witnessing is simply taking the initiative to share Christ in the power of the Holy Spirit and leaving the results to God."[3]

I think people understand the part about taking the initiative and the part about the Holy Spirit and leaving the results to God, but they often don't know what it means to "share Christ." We've already talked about normalizing spiritual conversation by simply talking about what God is doing in your life, what you're reading in the Bible, and how God responds to you in prayer.

But another key part of acting like others are Christians is being a *translator*, just like an ambassador to a foreign country. Essentially, when another person shares about their life, Christians can translate that experience into something already articulated in Scripture. In this way, you bring another person's experience into the framework of the Christian worldview. For example, a colleague of mine once asked if she could meet with me to discuss something important. She said, "I am wondering if you have a spirit-guide because I sense a powerful aura about you." Without hesitation, I said, "I do have a spirit-guide. His name is Jesus, and He indwells me by the Holy Spirit."

Another time, a neighbor invited me over to talk about her new interest in becoming a "Light Healer" as part of a New Age spiritual group. I immediately said, "Did you know that Jesus Christ was called the Light of the World and that He has power over darkness?" She was amazed. She asked me to show her where in the Bible Jesus is referred to in terms of light.

Christians are translators. We make one statement understandable in another language, in this case, the language of God's Word.

Sometimes, this work happens easily. I often sit with friends or colleagues and simply ask what they know about Jesus and the crucifixion, for example. People might say, "I'm not sure about Jesus. Didn't he commit some crime? Wasn't he some kind of radical?"

From a historical perspective, I'm able to answer questions—and translate misunderstandings—in these conversations. Sometimes these translation moments happen when friends try to explain to me something happening to them psychologically. People have often said something like, "The things I want to do, I don't do. I end up doing things I don't want to do instead. I don't understand myself at all!" In these moments, I can translate such statements into God's Word as articulated in Romans 7:15 where Paul makes the same desperate cry: "I do not understand what I do. For what I want to do I do not do, but what I hate I do." Here, Paul talks about the problem of sin; it's sin living in him that does this work. He ends that famous passage by saying, "What a wretched man I am! Who will rescue me? . . . Thanks be to God, who delivers me through Jesus Christ our Lord!" (vv. 24, 25). Friends who had visited psychics and astrologers sit there in shock that an ancient text could read their lives like this. Friends who feel so confused about their internal struggles cannot believe a man named Paul explained the battle they feel inside.

IT WASN'T THAT I WAS SO PERSUASIVE IN THAT MOMENT; IT WAS THAT JESUS WAS WORKING AND SHE NEEDED AN INVITATION TO RESPOND.

Again, Christians translate. A whole world is waiting for us to tell them what it is they are feeling and doing. It's as though they cry out, "What is happening to me? I don't understand what I'm doing!" And we come along and say, "I can help. I understand what's happening."

As I act like others are already Christians, I assume God is at work. I assume the audience wants to hear what I'm going to say. Therefore, I normalize spiritual conversations and translate experience in gospel language. As this happens, I'm asking Jesus to show me where He's working in this person's life and how I can help. I'm asking God to show me the right time to say, "What do you think about this? Do you think you would like to receive the free gift of salvation through Jesus Christ?"

I was sitting in my minivan with a neighbor who was struggling emotionally. We had been dear friends for several years—walking to school, eating pancakes, and dancing with children at our neighborhood fitness night. We had talked about Jesus all those years, but she continued to struggle with whether or not God was really good. She didn't know if she could trust Him to guide her life and care for her.

I turned to her and said, "Knowing Jesus is the best thing that could ever happen to you. Are you ready?" It wasn't that I was so persuasive in that moment; it was that Jesus was working and she needed an invitation to respond. We prayed in the van together, and when summer came, my husband baptized her. A few years later, her daughter followed her lead, receiving Christ and agreeing to a public baptism. Now, all these years later, she blesses our community with her life and art in a great ministry of compassion and service, especially to those who are grieving.

—◊◊◊—

So much time has passed in this little neighborhood. It's been eight beautiful, supernatural years. Every September, I feel like the work is finished and I'm ready for a new assignment. After all, our oldest, now a teen, walks herself to school. All the original children have grown, and some are graduating from high school. But every September, right as I stand in the driveway ready to discontinue this walk-to-school campaign, the Lord sends new families to love. Some are pushing strollers; some are new professors moving from across town; some are neighbors deciding to get some exercise.

So it all begins again.

I'm going to tell them what I'm learning about God today. I'm going to invite them to take a seat at the greatest table the world will ever know—in the heavenly realms with Jesus. As I think about being available and acting like people are already Christians, I'm amazed at how my life has changed from the time I was that girl at University of Virginia, crying on her dorm room floor. That young woman wanted abundant life. Instead of appearance, she found something to adore. Instead of affluence, she found she had access to the riches of Jesus. Instead of achievement, she learned how to abide. And now? Instead of the life she imagined, God gave her a small task in a small neighborhood.

And her life became bigger than she'd ever imagined.

I think about her as I read the words of Acts 20:24: "I consider my life worth nothing to me; my only aim is to finish the race and complete the task the Lord Jesus has given me—the task of testifying to the good news of God's grace."

It's a glorious task. It's a supernatural task that makes every day an adventure with Jesus.

SIT AND SAVOR

—∞—

Read 2 Corinthians 5.

1. Describe the last time you talked with another person about your faith in Jesus. What did you feel? Was it awkward, refreshing, difficult, easy? In what ways?

2. What's the biggest difference between how you talk to your Christians friends and your friends who do not yet know Jesus?

3. Turn to the person next to you and begin a conversation with the following prompts (or journal these answers):

   The last thing I read in Scripture that was really meaningful was:

   I have been praying about:

   God recently answered this prayer of mine in this way:

   Do you know what I love most about Jesus? I love:

4. What's the difference between trying to convince someone to know Jesus and sharing our experience with Him?

5. Share with the group or journal about the last time you shared your faith with someone openly. Then, share your own story of who first started talking to you about Jesus.

—ɯɯ—

MOMENT BY MOMENT

My hope is in you all day long.
— PSALM 25:5

A s you think about building a seated life, you may wonder how to live this reality in a daily kind of way. Just like my friend in the coffee shop, who, when I finished outlining this book for her asked, "How does one sustain that feeling of being seated?" I need to understand how to call forth my seated identity every day. It's a mindset one must practice.

When you experience yourself as seated at God's royal table, with specific good works appointed for you to do, you apply that truth to your day in a continual mindset. This mindset has become nearly cliché in our household because we use the expression "seated in Christ" so much. For example, our younger daughter comes home from choir practice filled with jealousy toward her best friend who always gets chosen to sing every solo.

Kate lounges in her bedroom as I fold some laundry beside her. "Tell me about what's going on," I say casually. She's like a little forest creature I could spook if I approach her too quickly or with too much intensity. When she tells me all about the jealousy, I move into Ephesians 2:6 by saying, "What if that's her special seat in Christ—to be the soloist, to be the star of the show? What

179

then? What if God never allows you to be the star? How would you handle that?"

Kate says, "I know she's seated too. And I'm seated. I know that. I know that God has great plans for my life, too. I do know that." She's nodding her head in recognition of the truth. "Sometimes I wish I had a different seat, but I know that my seat is good."

I know my seat is good.

We work through the emotions of it all—the jealousy, the low self-esteem, and the fear that she'll never be the best at anything—but in the end, we go back to that seat in the heavenly realms. *I know my seat is good.*

We have this kind of conversation several times during the week, and I must admit to you that it's not just a conversation to ease preteen jealousy and competition. I have the following conversations in my mind throughout the day:

When my plans change and I'm disappointed, *I know I'm seated* in Christ and God knows the plans for my day. When I begin to become fearful because of a new expense or bill payment, *I know I'm seated* in Christ and have full access to God's resources. I go to Jesus, trust Him to provide, and experience increasing peace. When I see another woman succeed or enjoy a particular blessing, I rejoice with her special seat in the heavenly realms. When I worry that I'm going to fail at a task set before me, *I remember I'm seated in Christ* with good works prepared in advance for me to do.

If I fail, God is in control. If I succeed, God is in control. When I want affection or attention—any kind of acknowledgment—I fix my eyes on Jesus and know that I have the attention of the almighty God who covers me with His righteousness. I know that I can approach the throne of grace with confidence and have all the affection, attention, and acknowledgment of the Most High God.

What happens as I go about my day and begin to regret my past or agonize over any painful memory? I think of God's sovereign plan that drew me to my seat in the heavenly realms. In this special seat, I can take my pain to Jesus and allow Him to turn that terrible thing into a beautiful thing. At no time am I abandoned, accused, or beyond help. I'm safe in my seat with a loving God working healing on my behalf.

Sᴉɴ DOESN'T TAKE ME FROM MY SEAT; IT JUST TURNS MY FACE AWAY FROM JESUS. I TURN BACK TO HIM AND ENJOY MY SEAT AT THE TABLE ONCE MORE. AT NO TIME WAS I EXCLUDED, REMOVED, OR SHUNNED FROM THE TABLE.

But what if I mess up during this same day? When I sin—through attitudes, speech, or behavior—I confess to Jesus and experience new intimacy with Him. Sin doesn't take me from my seat; it just turns my face away from Jesus. I turn back to Him and enjoy my seat at the table once more. At no time was I excluded, removed, or shunned from the table.

What if the phone rings, and I'm invited to do something new that scares me? When I am called into new assignments, I remember the battle-ready knights who surround me with shield and sword. I'm seated at this great army's table, and we have the strategies and resources of angelic armies surrounding us (Psalm 34:7). God is my helper and no weapon forged against me will prevail, as promised in Isaiah 54:17.

When I feel rejected, ignored, or left out, I visualize my seat in the heavenly realms in Christ Jesus. I belong. I'm included. No matter what I'm feeling, I hold it up to the truth of being *seated*.

When I'm seated in Christ, I change. I embrace that I'm a new creation. I can say no to my flesh and my old self and "put on the new self" (Ephesians 4:24).

Seated people REPLACE:

Loneliness with belonging (Psalm 68:6)

Despair with deep joy and peace (Romans 15:13)

Affliction with health and flourishing (Psalm 10:17 and Psalm 52:8)

The self-life with a crucified life (Galatians 2:20)

The spirit of heaviness with a garment of praise (Isaiah 61:3)

Seated people TURN:

From jealousy and competition into security and interconnectedness (Psalm 16:5 and 1 Corinthians 12:27)

From confusion and wandering into purpose and mission (2 Corinthians 5:20)

From impurity and compromising into a desire for worthy, holy things (Psalm 119:37)

Seated people TRANSFORM:

From weak to strong (2 Corinthians 12:10)

From independent to dependent (Isaiah 50:10)

From condemned to accepted and forgiven (Romans 8:1)

From fearful to courageous (Deuteronomy 31:6)

From lukewarm to passionately devoted (Philippians 3:7–8)

From greedy to generous (Psalm 37:26)

From self-protective to vulnerable (2 Corinthians 6:13)

From addicted to self-controlled (Titus 2:12)

Seated people, by God's power, display the fruit of the Spirit—love, joy, peace, patience, kindness, goodness, faithfulness, gentleness, and self-control (Galatians 5:22–23 ESV).

I am learning that when I'm seated with Christ and in Him in the heavenly realms I replace self-importance with being satisfied with Christ's righteousness (Romans 5:17); I replace foolishness with God's wisdom (1 Corinthians 1:21); I replace a desire for more with the abundance of my circumstances (John 10:10); and I replace gossip, complaining, and negativity with speech that blesses and instructs (Isaiah 50:4).

Everything about me changes. I'm adoring and not agonizing over my beauty; I'm accessing the riches of God's kingdom instead of accumulating wealth; and finally, I'm abiding in Jesus instead of exhausting myself with achievement. I replace my fear of missing out with a deep assurance that I'm exactly where I'm supposed to be. Here, I'm available for the grand adventure this day will bring.

You are free. The seat you've been fighting for all your life awaits you.

Let Jesus take you by the hand and lead you there.

Take this seat afresh every single day of your life.

SIT AND SAVOR

—⚭—

Read Joshua 1:8.

1. What old attitudes and behaviors can you replace with new ones, because you know you're seated with Christ?

   When I'm seated in Christ,

   I can replace_____
   with_____

   I can replace_____
   with _____

   I can replace_____
   with_____

2. Describe the most boring and mundane parts of your day. How does being seated in Christ change how you think about these times?

3. What spiritual disciplines would you have to put in place in order to keep a "seated in Christ" mindset?

4. What happens during your day that threatens your "seated in Christ" mindset?

5. Write out a prayer to Jesus to thank Him for what it personally means to you to be "seated with Christ in the heavenly realms in Christ Jesus."

———〰———

The author blogs daily at *Live with Flair* www.livewithflair .blogspot.com. She compiled her 400 most popular blogs in a devotion book arranged by season called *Live with Flair: Seasons of Worship and Wonder* (CreateSpace: 2014). Visit *Live with Flair* for free devotional material and access to her book on writing, *How to Write with Flair.*

NOTES

Chapter 2: A Single Verb

1. *Bible History Online*, "Mealtime Customs in the Ancient World: Chairs," http://www.biblehistory.com.

2. Gaius Sallustius Crispus (Sallust), *Sallust: Conspiracy of Catiline* (England: J. Brodie, n.d.), 55. Most likely published in 50 BC.

3. Isidore Singer and Cyrus Adler, "Temple: Administration and Service," *Jewish Encyclopedia: A Descriptive Record of the History, Religion, Literature, and Customs of the Jewish People from the Earliest Times till Present Day*, (New York: Funk & Wagnalls, 1901), http://www.jewishencyclopedia.com/articles/14303-temple-administration-and-service-of. Here, we read that "half of the chamber extended outside the court to the 'hel,' a kind of platform surrounding the courts, which was considered as secular, in contrast to the sacred premises within, where the priests were not allowed to sit down."

4. Charles Spurgeon, "The Only Atoning Priest," *A Sermon delivered on Lord's Day Morning, February 4th, 1872, at the Metropolitan Tabernacle*, Newington, Sermon 1034:73, http://www.spurgeon.org/index/c18.htm.

5. Ibid., 73.

6. The first mention of the Round Table appears in writing from the French poet Robert Wace in *Roman de Brut* (c.1155) based on Geoffrey of Monmouth's *History of the Kings of Britain* (c. 1136) that describes the history and mythology of Great Britain.

Chapter 3: Where You Never Sat

1. Evan Davis, "Addressing the Chair," *BBC Radio, Evan Davis' Blog,* April 23, 2009, http://www.bbc.co.uk/blogs/legacy/today/evandavis/2009/04/addressing_the_chair.html. Used with permission.

2. Y. T. Uhls and P. M. Greenfield, "The Value of Fame: Preadolescent Perceptions of Popular Media and Their Relationship to Future Aspirations," *Developmental Psychology* (December 19, 2011), doi: 10.1037/a0026369.

3. Sharon Jayson, "Generation Y's Goal? Wealth and Fame," *USA Today* January 9, 2007, http://www.usatoday.com/news/nation/2007-01-09-gen-y-cover_x.htm.

4. Uhls and Greenfield, 1.

5. Ibid., 9.

6. As of March 2015, according to the "Top 15 Most Popular Social Networking Sites," data as derived from *eBizMBA Rank*, "a continually updated average of each website's *Alexa* Global Traffic Rank, and U.S. Traffic Rank from both *"Compete* and *Quantcast,"* http://www.ebizmba.com/articles/social-networking-websites, Facebook attracts 900 million users monthly and Twitter over 300 million users.

7. Alexander Jordan, et al, "Misery Has More Company Than People Think: Underestimating the Prevalence of Others' Negative Emotions," *Personality and Social Psychology Bulletin* 37 (2010):120–135.

8. Kennon Sheldon, Neetu Abad, and Christian Hinsch,"Two-Process View of Facebook Use and Relatedness Need-satisfaction: Disconnection Drives Use, and Connection Rewards It,"*Journal of Personality and Social Psychology* 100 (2011): 766–75.

9. Silvan Tomkins in *Shame and Its Sisters: A Silvan Tomkins Reader*, Ed. Eve Kosofsky Sedgwick and Adam Frank (Durham: Duke University Press, 1995), 148.

Chapter 4: Imagine the Round Table

1. Julian Jones, Jake Michie, Julian Murphy, and Johnny Capps, "The Coming of Arthur, Part Two," *Merlin* (Season 3, Episode 13), Shine TV, UK, Perf, Bradley James, BBC, December 4, 2010.

2. From Charles Morris's version of *King Arthur and the Knights of the Round Table*, modernized from Sir Thomas Malory's *Morte de Arthur* (Lippincott, 1891), 50.

3. *Hayden Planetarium Guide*, as quoted by Lorrie Moore in the front matter of her book *A Gate at the Stairs* (New York: Vintage, 2010). To confirm the source of this quote, I contacted the Hayden Planetarium staff. While they could not direct me to the original source, they said, "[the quote] is factually correct. The planetarium is a spherical space, with the floor mildly sloping upward. The images projected into the domed ceiling and upper part of the wall can be seen equally by everyone." Email to the author, October 25, 2014.

4. Gregory Hocott, PhD, email message to the author, February 24, 2015. This framework, according to Dr. Hocott, "is now subsumed under glory/fame, one of the four classical temptations of Thomas Aquinas ("Power, Wealth, Pleasure, and Glory"). Throughout history, these are the big temptations seeking to devour souls." Used with permission, *Family Counseling Center*, Ann Arbor, Michigan, www.fccannarbor.net.

Chapter 5: From Appearance to Adoration

1. Joan Greve, "Study: Kate Middleton Has a Perfect Nose," *Time*, June 27, 2014, http://time.com/2934203/kate-middleton-study-perfect-nose/.

2. Ibid.

3. According to the American Society of Plastic Surgeons on their website www.plasticsurgery.org, rhinoplasty costs, on average $4,500.00, but this does not include the fees for anesthesia, hospital costs, consultation, medications, and the surgeon's fee. Patients might pay over $15,000 for this procedure.

4. M. Peskin and F. Newell, "Familiarity Breeds Attraction: Effects of Exposure on the Attractiveness of Typical and Distinctive Faces," *Perception* (2004):147–57.

Chapter 6: From Affluence to Access

1. Hannah Whitall Smith, in the *God of All Comfort*, discusses the "false rests" that come from Robert Wilkinson's writing in his booklet *The Saints Travel to the Land of Canaan Wherein Is Discovered Seventeen False Rests Below the Spiritual Coming of Christ in the Saints. Together with a Brief Discovery of What the Coming of Christ in the Spirit Is; Who Is the Alone Rest and Center of Spirits*, by R. Wilkinson, A Member of the Army (London: Printed for Giles Calvert, at the Black Spread-Eagle at the West End of Pauls, 1648).

Chapter 7: From Achievement to Abiding

1. Early Church Fathers in Henry Wace's compilation.

2. Henri Nouwen, *In the Name of Jesus: Reflections on Christian Leadership* (New York: Crossroad, 1992), 30.

3. Tim Keller, *The Freedom of Self-Forgetfulness: The Path to True Christian Joy* (Nashville: Thomas Nelson, 1982), 31.

Chapter 8: Four Hard but Great Questions

1. Andre Dubus, "The Doctor," *The New Yorker* (April 26, 1969), 38.

Chapter 9: Available Living

1. Jorge Luis Borges, trans. Normal Thomas di Giovanni, "The Life of Tadeo Isidoro," *The Aleph and Other Stories* (New York: Dutton, 1970) as quoted by Javier Cercas, trans. Anne McClean, *The Anatomy of a Moment* (London: Bloomsbury, 2009), 8.

2. Stephanie Koons, "Fitness Begins at Home," *Centre Daily Times*, February 19, 2010.

Chapter 10: Seated and Sent

1. Various verses including

   John 3:16: "For God so loved the world that he gave his one and only Son, that whoever believes in him shall not perish but have eternal life."

   Romans 3:23: "All have sinned and fall short of the glory of God."

   Romans 6:23: "The wages of sin is death, but the gift of God is eternal life in Christ Jesus our Lord."

   Romans 5:8: "But God demonstrates his own love for us in this: While we were still sinners, Christ died for us."

   John 14:6: "I am the way and the truth and the life. No one comes to the Father except through me."

   John 1:12: "To all who did receive him, to those who believed in his name, he gave the right to become children of God."

2. Portions of this account are from Heather Holleman, "Where You Walk," *Worldwide Challenge*, April 2014,:34–37.

3. Bill Bright, "Success in Evangelism," http://www.cru.org/train-and-grow/classics/transferable-concepts/be-a-fruitful-witness.6.html.

ACKNOWLEDGMENTS

T hank you to those who encouraged me to share my encounter with Jesus through Ephesians 2:6, especially Blair Jacobson, my tireless and talented agent, and Judy Dunagan, my acquiring editor at Moody who read this manuscript early one morning and let it speak to her heart. Thank you. I'm thankful for the ministry of Cru and the staff who offered multiple platforms to speak and write on overlooked verbs in Scripture and inspired the possibility of a book. Special thanks to Sonya Hove who encouraged me to speak on my recovery from the false selves of appearance, affluence, and achievement, and to Gregory Hocott, PhD, with Family Counseling Center who aided this recovery. Jennifer and Collin Rich provided guidance along the way, and I'm thankful for their sacrifice of time—often late in the evening—to minister to me. I am filled with gratitude for all the neighbors who agreed to have their stories in print and encouraged me as a writer. Brooke and Brian Barnett and Linda Darlington offered prayers about writing and life that spanned many years. Thank you to Denise Bortree, who walked miles with me as I wrote this book, offering wisdom and encouragement (and gifts of coconut mocha coffee) and to Bec Shepski who brought delicious dinners so I could write more as my deadline approached. Thank you to my neighbors in Centre County who have walked to school all these years with me, especially Jennifer and Rob Kelly, the Caswells and the De Lorenzi family who maintained their zeal for neighborhood fitness and the walk-to-school campaign on the days when I lost energy. JoAnn and Erik Foley-DeFiore loved and encouraged our family all these years, and Andrea Babich provided insight and treasured guidance along with the passionate Italian mama, Monica Kenney. Thank you to my talented friend Deb Placky, whose recommendation to watch *Merlin* became a turning point in my life; to Heather Russell for her prayers and great care for our family; to April and Kai Yorke for their friendship; and to my cherished writing friend Faith McDonald, who pushed me to write again when I had almost given up hope and who said with this manuscript, "to make Jesus the hero" and not me. Thank you to Lauren Kooistra for caring for us all in too many ways to recount. My students, along with the English department at Penn State, continue to appreciate and encourage my delight in vivid verbs, and I am so thankful for the privilege of teaching writing at the college level. Thank you to our Calvary church friends—the Kings, the Nolds, the Sigels, the Mattys, the Harts, the Pannebakers, the Kopreviches—who have prayed for me and encouraged my writing, and especially Lisa Seibel for her powerful prayer about my being seated with Christ. Thank you to Kitty and Curtis Holleman, Martha Weaver, and Aunt B for all their love and support of my writing. Thank you to Sandy Mackin for her wisdom and counsel over the last several years as I struggled to embrace that I was seated in Christ. Thank you, Sarah and Kate, my radiant daughters, who allow me to share their stories in writing and on stage. They have brought more joy and laughter to my life than I ever thought possible. My big sister, Melissa Kish, a true encourager and wise teacher, has been a faithful and loving support as I wrote this book. Thank you to Mom and Dad for all their love, generosity, patience, and joyous living. Finally, thank you to my husband, Ashley, my best friend and partner in life and ministry who makes me laugh every day and who, when I wander far away, leads me back to my seat with Jesus.